HOW TO
BAG
A
RINO

HOW TO
BAG
A
RINO

GRAY DELANY & ZACH WERRELL

The Whiz Kids Who Brought Down
House Majority Leader
ERIC CANTOR

Edited by Harry Stein

978-0692519585

Published by

The Calamo Press

New York City | Washington DC

calamopress.com
Currente-Calamo LLC
2425 17th Street NW, Washington D.C. 20009
244 Fifth Avenue, Ste. D169, New York, NY 10001

To the grassroots activists of Virginia's Seventh Congressional District, who made this victory possible, and to those across America doing the hard work of freedom.

TABLE OF CONTENTS

INTRODUCTION

The news out of Virginia the evening of June 10, 2014 was beyond merely momentous, for many in the media it seemed almost too much to grasp. CBS breathlessly declared it possibly "the biggest political upset in modern primary history." "A political earthquake," CNN concurred. Fox and ABC called it "stunning," the local *Richmond Times-Dispatch* "seismic," the *Washington Post* "a completely befuddling upset that no one saw coming."

The sheer sense of disbelief in mainstream circles was perhaps best captured in a follow-up on the *Post's* political blog *The Fix* the next morning. As it dawned on the nation's capital that the powerful Republican House Majority Leader Eric Cantor had actually been beaten by "David Brat, an unknown and under funded economics professor, . . . jaws dropped, and dropped, and dropped until they hit the floor," the *Post* reported, setting off a blizzard of tweets among the political class, an amazing number of which repeated the same two words:

> HOLY CRAP DID BRAT REALLY BEAT
> CANTOR?! #VA07
> > -Drew Belsky (@DJB627)

> Holy crap: Eric Cantor succumbs to
> tea party challenge
> > -Andrew Kaczynski (@BuzzFeedAndrew)

Holy Crap. Eric Cantor loses to tea party challenger Dave Brat. http:// www.nbcnews.com/politics/elect...

-Sabrina Siddiqui (@SabrinaSiddiqui)

Holy crap RT @DKElections: Cantor outspent Brat $993k to $76k in last seven weeks. Not a typo. #VA07

-Igor Babic (@igorbobic)

Holy crap is right. RT @mxmooney Holy crap. #ericcantor lost his primary to a Tea Party challenger.

-Shushannah Walshe (@shushwalshe)

Holy crap. http://usat.ly/1pDqMKM via @usatoday

-Jessica Newman (@newmanj12)

Look north, #RVA. That mushroom cloud is named "Holy Crap Cantor Lost."

-Josh Conrad (@josh_conrad)

Holy crap, Eric Cantor just lost his primary!!! #TeaPartyLives

-Ben Larrabee (@Ben_Larrabee)

Cantor's colleagues on the Hill, friends and foes alike, were more shocked than anyone; for weeks he had been telling House colleagues he was up by 20 points. Representative Lynn Jenkins (R–KS) had just arrived at Del Frisco's Grille, a steakhouse near the White House, when she heard the news, and would later describe it as the worst birthday ever. At the same time, according to the *New York Times,* "An informal dinner party at the Georgetown apartment of Representative Nancy Pelosi of California, the Democratic leader, turned into a celebration."

Their reactions made perfect sense—because in the political universe people like this inhabit, Cantor's loss made none at all. A so-called "Tea Party" candidate wasn't *supposed* to knock off a pillar of the GOP Establishment, let alone one with the alleged political gifts and massive built-in advantages of an Eric Cantor. Wasn't money the mother's milk of politics? Hadn't Cantor spent more than five million dollars on the race—and Brat a mere fraction of that?

Under the circumstances, the outcome of the race had seemed so preordained that the *Congressional Quarterly's* headline on Primary Day was a no-brainer: "Eric Cantor, Lindsey Graham Face Tepid Opposition." The piece blithely concluded that both the majority leader and the incumbent South Carolina senator were so clearly "cruising to primary victories" that the only question was whether Graham, who was facing five challengers, would top the 50 percent threshold needed to avoid a runoff. This he did—easily. Eric Cantor? As *The Hill* chimed in that morning, while his opposition was scarcely worthy of notice, Cantor—like Graham—had "decided early that it was better to crush them rather than merely beat them."

Nor was the assessment any different over on Fox, where political reporter Carl Cameron also saw the result as a sure thing, noting in his roundup on the day's elections, almost as an afterthought, that "GOP Congressman Eric Cantor, the House majority leader, faces a tea party challenge from a guy named David Brat."

And who could blame them? No House majority leader had been beaten in a primary. Never. Not since 1899, when the position was created. But, as is so often the case, the assumptions on which the media's take was based were not merely off; they were the herd mentality writ large, reflecting a profound ignorance of—and contempt for—the values and beliefs of the people who actually do the voting.

But there were some who did see it coming—some who fully expected Dave Brat to humble Eric Cantor.

Let's start with the two of us, the authors of this book.

We were the campaign manager and deputy campaign manager of the Brat campaign—indeed, its only two paid staffers. We were also, respectively, 23 and 24 years old.

What did we have against Eric Cantor? Plenty—like, as it would turn out, most of the voters of the Seventh District. But let's start with the all-encompassing reason: He's a RINO. And not just a run-of-the-mill RINO, but one of the most noxious of the breed.

> **RINO** (n) Acronym, literally Republican In Name Only. Generally used to describe lickspittle Republicans who in key aspects of their public performance are all but indistinguishable from Democrats. While they sometimes talk a good game on free markets, in practice they are dedicated to cronyism and shady deal making, if not given to outright corruption. They tend to be sickeningly beholden to the left/liberal media, unduly concerned

with being invited to fashionable dinner parties, and quick to be embarrassed by Republicans deemed too aggressively conservative and/or principled.

That's *our* definition, by the way, not Merriam-Webster's, so feel free to take it as a pretty good indication of where we stand on the subject.

You want particulars? Start with John Boehner and Mitch McConnell. Or John McCain. Or Lindsey Graham. Boehner, *the leader of the supposed opposition party*, when pressed about the Clinton Foundation and Hillary Clinton's involvement in the Benghazi scandal, actually called both Bill and Hillary Clinton "good public servants" and "good people."

Any other questions about why it's nearly as crucial to defeat RINOs as Democrats?

The term RINO is of fairly recent vintage, reputedly first used by veteran New Hampshire political columnist John DiStaso in December 1992 in the *Manchester Union Leader*. In the wake of Bill Clinton's election to the White House, during what were dark days for conservatives in his state, as they were nationally, DiStaso observed that in the State House, "Republicans were moving out and the Democrats and 'RINOs' (Republicans In Name Only) were moving in."

We often hear (usually from RINOs) that the word is deeply divisive. The GOP, they say, must be a "big tent party," open to those of differing views and values. They complain that the term promotes the kind of internecine warfare that only helps the true adversary, liberal Democrats.

But it's funny, RINOs mainly talk about the big tent and putting aside differences when they're seeking the support of disaffected conservatives; who, by the way, when it comes right down to it, over the years, usually have swallowed hard and supported the party's nominee. But let a conservative or libertarian come looking for Establishment support after defeating a GOP moderate in a primary, and, over and over, the big tent is closed for business.

Mike Huckabee has been especially outspoken in his scorn for those on the right he deems disruptive. In a January 2014 Facebook post, he urged that RINO be "outlawed from the vernacular of the party," calling it "a pejorative term that questions the authenticity and orthodoxy of someone's party purity." He continued, "I've been called that myself, even though I fought in the trenches of Republican politics for over two decades. Even so, I would never pretend that I'm Lord over determining who the real Republicans are." Adding that conservatives should "be focusing on their real differences with the left, not committing fratricide," he noted: "Personally, I think someone who agrees with me 90 percent of the time is not my enemy."

Now, we should probably say right up front that we, too, recognize that absolute purity is an impossibility. And, no, we certainly don't want to give liberal Democrats a helping hand, either. The last thing this country needs is more Barack Obamas, Hillary Clintons, Nancy Pelosis, and Harry Reids choking the life out of the American Dream and corrupting our form of government. As a general rule, we subscribe to the oft-repeated proposition that in most elections it makes sense for conservatives to get behind the farthest right *electable* candidate—even if in some jurisdictions this might involve sustained nose-holding.

But, like innumerable other conservatives, we've learned the hard way that the "lesser of two evils" argument is often a trap—or, worse, a ruse, with conservatives ending up feeling they've been played for fools. Far too many times, those on our side have voted for substandard candidates simply because they had an (R) beside their names; and for far too long, the Republican elites have taken us for granted, thinking we had no place else to go. Arguably even worse, we've repeatedly voted for candidates who say all the right things on the campaign trail—only to turn into mealy-mouthed apologists for the status quo once they get into office.

Is that the fault of the moderates? Sure. They've gotten away with this kind of thing for so long they have every reason to believe we're the knuckle-draggers they like to call us behind our backs.

Little wonder countless conservatives have come to feel cynical about contemporary politics. The system seems so immune to change that many don't even bother to vote—and it's hard to argue that they don't have a point.

Still, there are millions of us—indeed, in the age of Obama, more than ever—for whom standing on the sidelines simply is not an option. Aware of how much is at risk if we lose, and of how much we've *already* lost, we remain fully committed to the fight.

Erick Erickson recently described the stakes on the web site *RedState* with both cleverness and clarity:

> Even in this Constitutional Republic, for two centuries the beacon of liberty the world over, individual freedom retreats under the mounting assault of expanding centralized power . . . . Fiscal and economic excesses, too long indulged, already have eroded and threatened the

greatest experiment in self-government mankind has known.

As conservatives:

> we challenge as unwise the course the leadership of both political parties have charted; we challenge as dangerous the steps they plan along the way; and we deplore as self-defeating and harmful many of the moves already taken. Dominant in their council are leaders whose words extol human liberty, but whose deeds have persistently delimited the scope of liberty and sapped its vitality. Year after year, in the name of benevolence, these leaders have sought the enlargement of Federal power. Year after year, in the guise of concern for others, they have lavishly expended the resources of their fellow citizens. And year after year freedom, diversity, and individual, local and state responsibility have given way to regimentation, conformity, and subservience to central power.

Only deep into his piece does Erickson reveal that these stirring words are not his own, but come from the preamble to the 1964 Republican Platform on which Barry Goldwater ran. Erickson had altered only a few words, including changing "Democrats" to "leadership of both political parties."

If the realization of how little has changed in more than fifty years can be disheartening, also remember that the Goldwater campaign, though unsuccessful (resulting in the Great Society and what liberals fondly recall as the apex of their power), ultimately taught us the important hard lessons about the real nature of politics, which made President Reagan and Reaganism possible.

The fact is, the struggle for the soul of the Republican Party has been going on for generations, with (as Jonah Goldberg points out) Robert Taft, Barry Goldwater, Ronald Reagan, and Newt Gingrich each in his time going at it, hammer and tongs, against a powerful and ruthless GOP Establishment represented by, in turn, Thomas Dewey, Nelson Rockefeller, Bob Dole, and George H.W. Bush.

That struggle has been especially intense in the last several election cycles. Even as the rise of the Tea Party saw a resurgent GOP retake the House in 2010, the accommodationist, business-as-usual wing of the party sees the grassroots uprising less as a cause for celebration than as a mortal threat to its stranglehold on *their* party and power. These entrenched power brokers have fought back with all the formidable weapons at their disposal, starting with money—massive amounts of it—and a media that, though hardly sympathetic to the GOP leadership, regards the Tea Party and conservatives with open loathing.

Unfortunately, this internecine warfare has not gone all that well for the good guys. Repeatedly, we principled, small government insurgents have seen ourselves baselessly smeared in the media as bigots—so much so that even some who once proudly identified as Tea Partiers have abandoned the label. Nor, in some cases, have we helped our electoral brand by supporting candidates who—while able to knock off party regulars in primaries—proved unprepared by temperament or experience to win in November. (See Christine O'Donnell in Delaware, Richard Mourdock in Indiana, and—especially—Sharon Angle in Nevada, whose hamhanded campaign ensured the survival of Harry Reid.)

Consider it the lesson of Sir Galahad of the Round Table who thought, "because my heart is pure, I shall prevail." Uh uh. In politics, being right is not enough to win—if it were, conservatives would never lose. Nor is it about being the best human being in the contest; again, conservatives would lose only very rarely. What really matters is smarts and organization.

All of which brings us to Eric Cantor—for in the wide world of RINOs, Eric Cantor is among the very worst of the worst.

How so? As we will see, Cantor's long career has been marked by innumerable examples of duplicity in the service of personal ambition and at the expense of the conservative cause. But let's start with this: "Cantor sabotages conservatives in quest for speakership" ran the headline on a 2014 story on the conservative *Daily Caller* website, documenting how in an effort to ensure that he would succeed Boehner, "House Majority Leader Eric Cantor is intentionally sidelining one of his own Republican committee chairmen—and the chairman's attempts to pass conservative reforms." The chairman in question was conservative stalwart House Financial Services Chairman Jeb Hensarling of Texas, whose credentials include having been scored the second highest pro-taxpayer member of the House by the National Taxpayers Union. The story detailed how Cantor, seeing him as a potential rival for the speakership, consistently undermined Hensarling's efforts to advance the conservative agenda, including scuttling Hensarling's moves to abolish Fannie Mae and Freddie Mac. Indeed, rather than give Hensarling a perceived victory by backing his conservative version of flood reform, Cantor actually teamed up with left-wing California Democrat Maxine "the Tea Party can go straight to hell" Waters to pass a bill more to liberals' liking.

Though typically Cantor's dirty dealing passed under the radar—certainly the mainstream press had no interest in what they saw as a fight among equally objectionable right-wingers—the *Daily Caller* noted that genuine conservatives were "furious."

The piece appeared on April 8, 2014, two months before the primary in Virginia's Seventh District. You can count us among those infuriated conservatives. Here was yet another reason why so many of us passionately believed Cantor had to be beaten—and why we were working so incredibly hard to make that seeming political miracle come to pass.

This book is a record of how that historic victory happened. Yet it is also intended as a kind of how-to, for the lessons we learned are applicable to other races.

After the victory, the media focused on our age, making much of the fact it had been engineered by a team roughly the same ages as Justin Bieber and Miley Cyrus. Media types are nothing if not lazy, and it was an easy angle.

If our youth figured at all in what happened, it's perhaps only because we were less jaded than some of our more world-weary elders, so found it easier to believe that the supposedly invulnerable Cantor could be taken; and it probably helped us endure endless weeks of eighteen-hour days, running on fumes and caffeine. Had we been much older, we would probably never have had the shot in the first place; not many who have families to support (and future employment to worry about) volunteer for supposed "suicide missions."

As things were, the campaign was a steep climb, featuring many rough patches and some real acrimony. But it brought together a group of people who stuck together to the end, and along the way we became a real band of brothers. We laugh today about how it was then—it's always easier to laugh in retrospect—but we like to say that we pledged our lives, our fortunes, and our sacred honor to getting Dave Brat elected. It was absolutely so.

Our aim, both in this book and in our electoral work going forward, is to continue doing more of the same, helping bring to office men and women committed to enlarging the sphere of freedom in America. And that starts with reclaiming the Republican Party.

In the next election cycle, and in the one after that, we hope to see ever growing numbers of astonished RINOs and their moderate supporters across the country surveying the wreckage on the morning after a race, exclaiming, in astonishment and distress, "Holy crap!"

ZACH: A LITTLE BACKGROUND

Some might call my goal in getting involved with politics a bit immodest: I wanted to alter the direction of this country. As far as I'm concerned, policy on both sides of the aisle is fatally flawed, and at first I assumed that the way to make the biggest impact would be to work directly on policy. But I was wrong. The real fast lane to political change is changing *who* makes policy.

Call it either a liability or my greatest asset, but I've always been a bit of a bomb thrower. Growing up in southern Maryland, a lot of the guys on my high school sports teams called me Crazy Werrell.

Curt Deimer

And my attitude? On the first day of sports practice, as a freshman, you should go out and punch the starting middle linebacker in the face just to show everybody you're not going to be messed with. By my senior year, I *was* the starting linebacker, weighing only 167 pounds–after which they moved me to defensive end. So "this cannot be done" has never been part of my calculus; in fact it makes me more recalcitrant.

Anyway, you can't worry about what other people think. If I believe in something, I'm going to play like a possessed wild animal, both in sports and politics. I stand up for what I believe with every ounce of my being.

It was in high school that I first got seriously engaged ideologically, watching Ron Paul in the presidential debates. He was a revelation–not only sparked my interest in libertarianism, but stoked my contempt for America's insufferably smug ruling elites.

A couple of years later, I was on one of the nation's most liberal campuses, where I was recruited to play lacrosse *and* was a conservative libertarian (two strikes against me), which is something I'd recommend to any young conservative or libertarian looking to someday do his part in bringing down the left. In my case it was Haverford College, and my four years there not only sharpened my skills but, I like to think, proved to my classmates that not only is a Tea Party person not necessarily a "hater," but can also have an intelligent and informed position. And –unlike so many–can actually engage in civil discourse.

My senior thesis was on the role that national, state and local economic conditions have on presidential elections, and in December 2012, during my senior year, I went to the GOP convention in Maryland, the state where I was raised. The MDGOP was putting on a number of seminars in conjunction with the convention, and at one of them the speaker was giving a presentation on how to frame issues in a campaign, and he was discussing all these hardcore free market Austrian economists I admired but almost nobody else seemed to know. So afterward, I went up to him. He looked me over in some surprise–I was the only "kid" there wearing a three-piece suit, like he was–and when he asked for my résumé, I handed him one…on *paper.* "Wow," he said, "nobody has paper résumés anymore. I like you. You're coming up for lunch with me in D.C. next week."

His name was Chris Doss, of the Leadership Institute, and he became my mentor in this industry. After I graduated, he got me into the Leadership Institute's Campaign Management School, which offers a week-long crash course in the nuts and bolts of running a campaign. Soon after, Chris landed me my first political job: working for a Tea Party Republican in a race for Virginia's House of Delegates.

Our guy, Mark Berg, a doctor, ran hard against Obamacare, and after first knocking off a sitting Republican moderate in the primary, we smoked the Independent in the general. We took 65 percent (64.97 percent…but who's counting?) of the vote, including all but one precinct in Winchester, the district's biggest and most liberal city.

By then, I knew this was exactly where I belonged. True, any illusions about it being a sexy job were long gone. Campaign politics is a grind: four-plus months of sixteen- to twenty-hour days filled with data collection, voter contact, and voter identification–the "glorified bean counting of politics," as I like to dismissively describe my job–and otherwise scrapping with every ounce of your being with a work ethic largely unknown to my generation to get the word to the voters, and then get the voters to the polls.

The sexy part is winning.

GRAY: A LITTLE BACKGROUND

Growing up in Charlottesville, Virginia, my family was conservative, though not especially political. But I caught the bug early. My first campaign was 2004, Bush's reelection, when I was in the ninth grade. I didn't do much–worked the polls, helped out a bit at the local Republican Party headquarters–but I was hooked. And there was no question where I stood: Republicans = Good, Democrats = Bad.

I no longer feel quite the same way today. Don't get me wrong; Democrats *still* = Bad, maybe more so than ever. But these days, as far as I'm concerned, Establishment Republicans = Not Much Better. Arrogance and cronyism are rampant in *both* parties.

I learned all I needed to know about wishy-washy, unprincipled,  cynical mainstream Republicanism when I went to work for Linda McMahon in her 2012 Senate race in Connecticut. It was my first job out of the University of Richmond, and I was put in charge of her field office in Waterbury, one of the most economically depressed towns in America. The economy was so terrible in Connecticut that Linda actually had a shot. And as the cofounder, with her husband Vince, of World Wrestling Entertainment, she had more money than God. In fact, up until early October, she was polling well.

What she needed to win was to campaign on all the terrible damage the Democrats had done to that state and stand unequivocally for the opposite: conservative small government. She needed to propose specific programs to be cut and income tax reductions necessary to create a more business-friendly environment. And she needed to tell the truth: that politicians, of either party, who promise the moon are peddling a load of crap.

In short, she needed to give voters credit for having functioning brains, and treat them that way.

So what did they do instead, these geniuses running her campaign? They fell back on the GOP Establishment's playbook. Since Connecticut is a "liberal" state, they tried to outpander the Democrats, as if that's humanly possible. The message became not only is Linda *not* Tea Party, she's not even *really* conservative. They actually started running spots of people saying, "I'm voting for Barack Obama *and* Linda McMahon—because Linda McMahon cares." They put out literature linking Linda and Obama even more closely—and then distributed it only in minority neighborhoods.

It was sickening, a totally fraudulent, BS campaign that believed in nothing and treated voters, and especially minority voters, like sub-morons.

Naturally, our base was furious. Out where I was, people saw this crap and started ripping down their pro-Linda signs, and telling me there was no way they were going to vote for her. When I'd report this to higher ups, the attitude was: "Where else are they gonna go? Are they going to vote for a Democrat?"

Well, on Election Day, a lot of them didn't go anywhere—including out of their homes to vote. The Democrat won by 12 points.

The bottom line? Desperate as it is to win elections, the Republican Establishment has zero interest in what drives the rest of us—changing the culture and setting the course of the country.

ONE

ERIC CANTOR:
CONSERVATIVE RATING, F-MINUS

For Democrats and liberals—and even for those on the right who don't follow politics closely—the scorn with which many conservatives viewed Eric Cantor was a mystery. After all, based on everything they heard, wasn't Cantor a full-fledged, unapologetic, even *Tea Party* conservative? Indeed, he was supposedly one of the great hopes of the Republican Party going forward—bright, attractive, well-spoken, sharp. A "young gun," part of "a new generation of conservative leaders" as he and co-authors Paul Ryan and Kevin McCarthy dubbed themselves in their 2010 bestseller. (Fellow "young gun" McCarthy would replace Cantor as majority leader when Cantor was left for political dead after Dave Brat proved a little faster on the draw.)

The image was no accident. Cantor had worked studiously to project it even before his election to Congress in 2000. In fact, this was a guy who'd *always* had his eye on the prize; the sort who from day one makes sure to punch all the right buttons. Going to the right schools—starting with Richmond's tony Collegiate School—he made all the right connections. While an undergrad at George Washington University, he interned with Tom Bliley, the longtime congressman in Virginia's Seventh District, and served as his driver. Before 30, Cantor was in the Virginia House of Delegates (where his aggressively pro-corporate views got him nicknamed "Overdog"), and when Bliley unexpectedly announced in 2000 he wouldn't seek an eleventh term, Cantor was the first to jump into the race to succeed him.

Then as now, in the solidly Republican Seventh Congressional District, winning the primary was tantamount to winning the seat. That year, the primary was very hotly contested—and equally dirty—but with Bliley's support, Cantor pulled through by 254 votes.

Nothing very unusual in any of that—Congress is full of hyper-ambitious opportunists who have been dreaming big since back in the days of middle school student council. The question, in Cantor's case, is how he rose so quickly from the new kid on the block to the upper echelons of party leadership.

Let's give him his due. Partly his success came because he's smart, something far less common in the upper reaches of government than we might wish. Moreover, he has a rare talent, even a gift, for cultivating those above him on the ladder: Some might call it brownnosing. But the number one reason is dollars—lots and lots of them. From the start, Cantor proved himself a phenomenal fundraiser. He founded Eric PAC (standing for Every Republican Is Crucial) in

2002, which in the first two years alone, raised over a million dollars. The money was cannily, if not wisely, spent; used to buy the goodwill of other Republicans. That was just the start. It is estimated that by 2014, Cantor had raised over $30 million.

Of course, as these things always go, that money came with plenty of strings attached. The bulk of Cantor's cash came from Wall Street, and much of that from BlackRock, which bills itself the world's largest asset manager.

Any wonder why Cantor soon emerged as one of the political world's leading crony capitalists?

These people were not just professional associates; they were his crowd, the ones he liked to hang with, and all the more so as his power grew. As the *Weekly Standard*'s Andrew Ferguson has observed:

> "A seldom-remarked fact of American politics is that people in positions of governmental authority—senators, cabinet officers, governors, ranking members of the House of Representatives, Republicans and Democrats alike—live a life utterly removed from that of the people they rule, with cars and drivers and private jets on call, sumptuous meals and skyboxes stocked with excellent liquor, all for free. They will tell you it's to make the people's business run more smoothly, but they also think it's fitting compensation. Why else would they put up with the rest of us?"

In Cantor's case, he had a preference for the Hamptons, and jetting off to the World Economic Forum in Davos, Switzerland.

Nor, along the way, was he doing so badly for himself personally, either. Based on a rough 2013 estimate by the transparency watchdog Open Secrets, during his time in Congress, Cantor's net worth increased from $1 million to $19.7 million. And that estimate is likely very low, since the reporting rules governing such things are intentionally lax. As *Politico* has observed, "It is impossible to truly know how wealthy members of Congress are because they are only required to disclose assets and liabilities in broad ranges." We do know this: Cantor's pay as a congressman topped out at $193,400—and then only after he became majority leader.

So how did he get away with it for so long? A lot of it was old-fashioned branding: Cantor the young gun, who went out of his way to present himself as a no-nonsense champion of the little guy on talk shows, television commercials, and press releases. Then there was the media. Reporters tend to be not just lazy, economically illiterate, and incurious about the way Congress really works, but especially ignorant about conservatives and conservatism, pretty much regarding the entire right as Neanderthaland.

In Cantor's case, the mainstream media readily bought his self-generated image as an unwavering conservative. Cantor's hometown paper, the *Richmond Times-Dispatch*, called him the "high-visibility point man for Republican resistance to President Barack Obama on issues such as taxes, deficit reduction and health care." Indeed, in 2012, much of the media blamed the bitter debt ceiling negotiations on, as NPR had it, "Cantor's no-compromise tactics . . . and his fiercely loyal Tea Party-fueled caucus members."

In fact, the ruse was so effective that for a time even the Tea Party bought it. After all, few in Congress *talked* so persuasively about the need for deregulation and smaller government; besides which—

the ultimate merit badge for conservative good conduct—Obama despised him. And why not? Hadn't Cantor been so firm holding the line on raising taxes in the 2011 negotiations preceding the sequester that Joe Biden finally walked out on him?

Yet even then, for anyone who bothered to look closely, Eric Cantor was one of the poster boys for all that was rotten in the modern Republican Party, a man who took on the protective coloring of honest conservatism to rise (and personally profit) in public office, while quietly pursuing the classic RINO path of accommodation with big business and behind-the-scenes surrender to big-government Dems.

Including on the debt—where in the end, he caved.

And on Benghazi, where he and Boehner were the two responsible for long blocking an investigation into the malfeasance that led to the tragedy.

Where voters were concerned, Cantor had one overriding aim: Make sure they focus on what I say, not on what I do.

When did the realization of who this guy really was finally sink in? It began to happen in the district long before it happened nationally. The conservative activists in the Seventh District are pretty savvy to start with, and of course they were keeping a lot closer eye on their guy than the Washington herd—and more and more evidence was piling up that he just reeked of phoniness.

The first major tipoff was back in 2008 with his support for TARP—aka the Wall Street bailouts. It signaled the extent to which Cantor was in bed with those who cared more about lining their own pockets than the welfare of the country. If banking executives' taking taxpayer money and TARP funds—along with bonuses rebranded as "retention payments"—wasn't bad enough, among the chief banks chosen to be bailed out, even while so many community banks went under, was Goldman Sachs, where Cantor's wife Diana happened to have previously worked.

Indeed, Eric and Diana Cantor were the ultimate power couple--*real* power, not the empty kind celebrated in *People* magazine. Diana sat on multiple corporate boards, where there tended to be something of a gap between the compensation and the workload. As the *National Journal* observed in 2013 of the labors of Mrs. Cantor on behalf of Domino's Pizza, "Domino's has delivered cash, stock and stock options currently worth more than $3 million to Diana Cantor since October 2005—all for her part-time work as a director." Meanwhile, she was simultaneously working for the Virginia Retirement System, in charge of funneling Virginia Retirement System money to selective hedge funds and banks on Wall Street. Asked by the magazine to comment on his wife's relationship with Domino's, Cantor blandly replied: "I'm very proud of Diana, who over the past thirty years has built a tremendous business career while raising our three wonderful children. She is an example to all aspiring young women and working mothers who want to study hard, work hard, and achieve great things."

Small banks certainly weren't too big to fail, and family businesses did not get bailed out—just Cantor's friends. It stank to high heaven.

Then there were his votes on the debt. Through the Bush years and up into the Obama administration, Cantor voted to raise the debt ceiling ten out of fourteen times--and the only times he voted against it were the years Republicans were in the minority, meaning there was no question it would pass anyway, meaning those brave "no" votes were just for show. When it counted, *he folded every time*, voting against the people—and for Wall Street.

The Three Amigos   *Corbis*

The truth is, Cantor had little more interest in reducing spending than liberal Democrats. For a guy like Cantor, as for other RINOs, fiscal responsibility is a pose; the hard votes show that his heart was never in it. There's no way it would happen on his watch, especially not if it meant facing up to an ideologue like Obama.

But what truly exposed Cantor for who he is was the creation, in 2010, of Heritage Action, as the lobbying arm of the Heritage Foundation. Heritage Action began scrutinizing legislators' votes on key conservative measures, looking at the fine print of amendments and paying particular attention to measures where crony capitalism might be at play—those that enabled supposedly red meat conservative legislators to screw their constituents while quietly feathering their own nests. In brief, Heritage Action started snooping around in what might be called Cantor World.

Eric Cantor's Heritage Action score turned out to be a lowly 53 percent.

You read that right. The House majority leader received an F– from one of America's leading conservative groups. With Republican leadership like that, who needs Democrats?

Around the same time, *60 Minutes* ran a segment on the Stop Trading on Congressional Knowledge Act—the "STOCK Act"—designed to curtail the appalling, yet longstanding, practice whereby members of Congress traded on insider knowledge. For instance, if the Pentagon was about to purchase 500,000 BlackBerry smartphones, it had hitherto been entirely legal for a member of Congress to buy BlackBerry stock based on that knowledge. This new legislation was supposedly designed to curtail this abuse, which, of course, would land any ordinary citizen in jail. Once Obama signed the legislation, the matter seemed settled.

Except three months later, it came to light that just before passage, a certain powerful congressman—guess which one—had inserted an amendment into the bill, garbling its language, thereby allowing *family members* to continue trading on congressional knowledge:

> "Cantor's office insisted it did nothing to change the intent of the STOCK Act. But when pressed with the new information uncovered by CNN, the majority leader's office conceded it made changes to the House bill that effectively took out the requirement for spouses and children to file these reports."

Arrogant? The term doesn't begin to do Cantor justice.

Meanwhile, as Cantor's power and celebrity grew, he paid less and less attention to his own district, rarely bothering to make the two-hour drive south to attend festivals or town halls; when he did, he rolled up in a fleet of black SUVs with tinted windows. Cantor was far more likely to be fundraising in Los Angeles or the Hamptons than in Hanover or Henrico. If you were lucky enough to gain entry to a town hall, you were not allowed to ask questions.

By 2014, on the eve of Dave Brat's campaign, Cantor was as isolated from his constituency as Nicholas II was before the Russian Revolution—and equally surrounded by yes-men, ever ready to reassure him that everything was fine.

Rumblings of discontent in the district? The possibility of a serious challenge? Nothing to worry about—just a few right-wing nut job peasants.

GRAY'S TAKE

I started turning against Cantor in 2011, when I spent six weeks working as a summer intern in his Washington office. He had a couple of young legislative assistants, one of whom was a graduate of Cantor's old prep school, Collegiate, whose upper-crust parents had hooked them up with Cantor. Supposedly, their job was constituent service, which, theoretically, is high on every congressman's agenda. But it wasn't even on their radar. Like so many people in the D.C. bubble, they were self-important jerks. They would kick back all day drinking Starbucks, maybe attend a few committee hearings, then spend the rest of the day shooting the breeze about fantasy football, and not caring a lick about helping people. It was truly shocking. What mattered to them was only whether they'd be going to the Capitol Hill Club that night–and whether someone "important" might be there.

If I, or one of the other starry-eyed interns, would say, "I've got a constituent on the line with a legitimate question, could you please take this?" they'd tell us to put the call through to voicemail–and then never call back. The caller would instead receive the dreaded constituent letter that didn't answer the question–yet that allowed the office to check a box indicating the moron constituent had been helped. Or sometimes we'd just be told to lie to people to get them off the phone.

At one point, during the "tense" budget negotiations with Joe Biden, the policy director made a show of asking us for our recommendations for deficit reduction. He encouraged us to find recently created programs that would be easier, politically, to kill. We spent a considerable amount of time on the project. I offered a number of proposals, including eliminating a recently created HUD program. The policy director thanked me, but clearly nothing was going to come of it, or of anyone else's suggestions. Lip service, not action, is the coin of the Establishment's realm.

Of course, it was Cantor who set the tone. And because Cantor treated everyone around him like a peon, there were no consequences when his staff did the same. Indeed, Cantor's treatment of his interns was telling: There we were, working long hours for free, yet never once did he come over to chat or even shake our hands.

In the grand scheme of things, these might seem like minor matters, and complaining about them might even sound petty. But they were hugely telling about the real man behind the one parading his ego on the network news.

TWO

"ELECTABLE!"

Recruiting a credible conservative to take on Eric Cantor in a primary was no easy task. To everyone who "mattered"—the political establishment, journalists, deep-pocketed GOP donors—Cantor was bulletproof. Such a race was widely deemed not just unwinnable, but foolhardy—a likely career-killer.

The intimidation factor can hardly be overstated. In the upper reaches of the Republican Party, Cantor was the political equivalent of a Mafia don. He wielded power with cold efficiency, punishing those who got out of line even as he dispensed largesse to the favored.

Yet in the very heart of his power base, Virginia's Seventh District, were a handful of conservative activists who, soon after the 2012 elections, set about finding someone with the potential to knock him off.

What made them believe that Cantor could be taken down?

Start with Floyd Bayne.

Floyd was the guy who had dared challenge Cantor in the June 2012 primary, and it was easy to dismiss him as little more than a sacrificial lamb. He was portrayed as a nothing, a substitute teacher with no political experience. Despite a valiant effort on his part, he garnered just 20.6 percent of the vote—which Cantor held up as a drubbing.

But it depended on how you read the numbers—and, almost by definition, grassroots activists are glass-half-full types. What they saw was that Floyd was a great guy but a flawed candidate. Despite being absolutely correct on the issues, his résumé and appearance made dismissing him all too easy. To top it off, he had almost no campaign at all; no money, little organization or advertising, really not much of anything.

Yet for all that, he took *21 percent*! More than *a fifth*!

What that indicated, for those willing to see, was that there was a floor: You could run a sock monkey against Eric Cantor, and you'd start with a fifth of the vote.

Listening to Floyd's speeches now, what's striking is that his message wasn't all that different from the one Dave Brat would win with. It just wasn't as focused; hadn't yet been distilled to go down smoothly. It was still mash instead of whiskey.

Remember Sir Galahad? Being right is not enough to win.

For anti-Cantor activists in the Seventh, the results in the general that November were even more telling. Wayne Powell, the Democrat, ran a smart campaign. He may have been a raving liberal, dead wrong on just about every issue that mattered to conservatives, but he wasn't going to let the voters know it. Indeed, his signature radio ad made him sound more like a Tea Party guy. Featuring a pair of old folks with Virginia twangs, (the liberal stereotype of typical conservative voters), it began with the sound of hammering:

Tom: Hey, Herb, see ya puttin' up your Romney sign.

Herb: Just like you, Tom.

Tom: How ya votin' for Congress?

Herb: Oh, the usual—Eric Cantor.

Tom: Well, what do you like about Eric Cantor, Herb?

Herb: Well, he . . . uh . . . uh . . .

Tom: Is it how he ran the coin-operated Congress? Taken over two and a half million bucks from big banks and investors?

Herb: He did?

Tom: Well, maybe you like how he strongly supported that budget that cut taxes for corporations that sent jobs overseas instead of makin' things here.

Herb (drily): No, that wouldn't be it.

Tom: So what *is* it you like about Eric Cantor?

Herb: Well, he's a Republican, isn't he?

Tom: No, Herb, you and I are Republicans. Eric Cantor works for himself and his corporate sugar daddies. Let me let you in on a little secret: I'm voting for Wayne Powell, the candidate who's not for sale.

Herb: Well, if you promise not to tell anybody, I'm gonna vote for Powell, too.

Tom: Now, who would I tell?

Announcer: Wayne Powell for Congress. Because this election isn't about red and blue, it's about red, white, and blue.

On November 4, Cantor beat Powell by 58 percent to 41 percent, but that 17-point margin was Cantor's smallest in a general election yet. He had won all his previous races by at least 25 points

Moreover, as the ad noted, 2012 was a presidential year, Romney versus Obama, who was exceedingly unpopular in the overwhelmingly Republican Seventh.

But if the 2012 results offered a measure of hope, they also reaffirmed how difficult mounting such a campaign would be—and it would start with finding the right candidate. Clearly, if such an individual were to have even a ghost of a chance, the candidate would have to be someone who had not just the guts to stand up to the retribution of Cantor and his powerful supporters, but a résumé and personal style that would impress both the general electorate and those needed to finance the campaign—Richmond's upper-crust donor class.

A little more than a month after the 2012 election, Kim Singhas, a skilled grassroots organizer known to have her finger on the district's pulse, received a call from fellow conservative activist Gerry Baugh, an auto body shop owner in Henrico County and head of the local Tea Party. A fellow "early adopter"—as they termed themselves—in the campaign to rid the nation of Eric Cantor, Baugh wanted her to meet a guy named Dave Brat.

The name wasn't entirely unfamiliar to Singhas. Brat was the head of the economics department at Randolph–Macon College in nearby Ashland, and though he had never held political office, he had served as a legislative assistant to a Virginia state senator; and the year before, he had unsuccessfully sought the Republican nomination for a seat in the state House of Delegates.

As Kim approached and saw Brat standing in front of Baugh Auto Body, a single word leaped to mind: *Electable.* "He was tall, attractive, well dressed," she recalls. "He *looked* like a congressman."

That impression was confirmed, and then some, as the three of them talked over noodles at the Mekong Vietnamese restaurant next door. "He was bright, obviously—had a Ph.D. in economics—but just as important, he was charismatic. *Electable.*"

At one point, when Dave was out of earshot, Baugh turned to her and nodded his agreement: "He's the real deal."

Kim spent the rest of the two-hour lunch giving Dave the hard sell: "I ran the numbers, precinct by precinct. I said, 'Dave, we can absolutely take him if you run to the right of him. It's an off-presidential year; there's nothing else on the ballot—we can take him.'"

Brat had already discussed the possibility with others, and it was clear he had some interest. At the same time, "reading the non-verbals," Kim sensed he would take a lot more convincing.

Indeed, midway through Kim's pitch, he leaned across the table and offered what he seemed to think might be a dealbreaker: "He looked me right in the eye and said, 'You know, I'm a libertarian. I'm a Republican, but really I'm a libertarian.'"

She reassured him that this was not an issue; there was room in the party for libertarians—though if he were going to win, he'd have to run as a conservative libertarian, a conservative populist, or the now in vogue "conservatarian."

But an even greater concern for Brat was the potential impact of such a race on his reputation, his career and his family.

Brat knew even better than most what the House majority leader and his minions were capable of, for he had something of a personal history with Cantor. It involved his abortive 2011 attempt to secure the GOP nomination for the House of Delegates. There were four candidates, of whom Dave was clearly the most qualified. But among the others was the 26-year-old son of the head of a huge energy company, Dominion Resources, and—no surprise—Cantor's organization skirted democratic procedures to select the inexperienced kid as the candidate. No primary, no convention, not even an open meeting—just a panel of GOP honchos. Afterward, they put out a statement loaded with the usual Establishment language about "expanding the base" and "making the party a big tent," and how the kid was the best choice to do that.

Dave is nothing if not honest—he taught ethics as well as economics—and he was shocked and infuriated seeing first-hand the depth of the corruption within the Virginia Republican Party. It couldn't be clearer that they were committed to retaining their hold on power, and weren't shy about using outright thuggery to get it done.

If not for that experience, it's an excellent bet he would never have run against Cantor.

But that's only part of the story. The rest involves the previous holder of that disputed seat in the House of Delegates, Cantor ally Bill Janis, and a close friend of Dave Brat's named Matt Geary. In 2011, after Geary won the Republican nomination for Henrico County Commonwealth Attorney, the Virginia Republican Party moved to take over his campaign. He was expected to go with the party's chosen campaign manager, direct mail vendor, and so forth. An independent guy, Geary said thanks—but no thanks. Infuriated, the Establishment decided to teach him a lesson. Rather than support the party's popularly chosen nominee, Geary, the Establishment machine—nicknamed "The Henrico Mafia" or "The Family"—violated its own rules and recruited Janis to run against Geary as an independent, giving him massive financial backing. The party then leaked word to the media that Geary had had an affair—and, as day follows night, Cantor's allies on the Henrico County Republican Committee declared Geary morally unfit, and demanded that he leave the race in favor of Janis. Indeed, many voters still remember that campaign as being about supposed "deadbeat dad" Geary. Though a devastated

Geary publicly conceded the truth of the affair—by then ended—and even after moving out of his home, he refused to quit the race.

In November, both Janis and Geary lost to the Democrat. Two months later, the following appeared on page one of the *Richmond Times-Dispatch*:

Matthew Geary, Former Henrico GOP Candidate, Found Dead

Prominent attorney Matthew P. Geary, whose candidacy for Henrico County's chief prosecutor rattled the establishment but ended in defeat two months ago, was found dead Sunday from what police said was a self-inflicted gunshot wound. Geary, 42, was found by family members who notified police about 1 p.m. Sunday . . . Geary's campaign ran into trouble after a highly orchestrated attack on his character by Republican leaders, including Eric Cantor, R–7th, and Henrico Republican Party figures, who revealed that Geary had had an affair with a married woman in recent years.

Geary fully admitted to the affair but said it had ended, yet political opponents used the relationship to attack Geary's judgment and responsibility, supporting instead longtime Henrico Del. Bill Janis, who abandoned years of work in the General Assembly to take on Geary. Geary refused to abandon his campaign, despite a public request that he do so by the county Republican Committee . . .

Another piece, in Richmond's *StyleWeekly* magazine, added a couple of poignant, telling, details: Geary had five children "and deeply regretted hurting them . . . . 'I had to leave home for what I'd done,' Geary said he told his children. Geary moved out of the family's house while remaining active in their lives, his friends say. But his troubles, it turns out, became too much to bear."

So Dave Brat had no illusions about what taking on Cantor could mean. Both he and his wife Laura, who had been close to the Gearys, knew they would have to deal with *House of Cards*–style politics—ruthless, brutal, and anything goes.

Kim wasn't surprised that Brat left the meeting without committing. It was, after all, still nearly a year and a half until the primary.

In the months that followed, Brat mulled it over, working his Rolodex, making phone calls, sounding out others about the possibility. Notably, he found enthusiastic support for the idea from former Senator Jim DeMint, president of the hugely influential Heritage Foundation, as well as Larry Nordvig, former head of the Richmond Tea Party. Other Tea Party groups in the district also seemed supportive.

After calling occasionally to keep in touch, Kim heard from him on March 25, 2013, by email: "I have some good news for you," he reported.

Still, he let her know he was not ready to go public with the decision.

As far as the world was concerned, this meant there was no challenger to Cantor. But that changed in November 2013, when one appeared out of nowhere: Pete Greenwald, a retired Naval officer who taught ROTC at James River High School.

Concerned, Kim Singhas wanted a look at Greenwald. A few weeks later, she attended an event at the Mechanicsville Tea Party, where he was the guest speaker. She was unimpressed. Though Greenwald is an extremely nice fellow with a valiant military record, deeply involved in the community and clearly a staunch conservative, he was awkward on the stump, and not quite ready for prime time. Commander Greenwald might well have a future in politics, but this wasn't the right race or the right time.

The next day Singhas shot off an email to Dave Brat:

Last night we had a planted question in the audience to Pete Greenwald: "If another candidate were to enter the race who was well funded and had name recognition and electability would you drop out?" Pete said yes he would consider it—"it's not about me—it's about WINNING," meaning defeating Cantor and electing a conservative.

He's a good guy—TOTALLY UNELECTABLE—but could be an asset as a veteran working veterans groups and the military vote for YOU.

At the gathering, Kim had spread the word that before committing to Greenwald, people should be aware that there was another candidate who would be getting into the race.

"Really need to sit down with him ASAP," she added in her note, "before he peels away volunteers."

Finally, a month later, on January 7, 2014, five months and three days before the primary, Dave pulled the trigger.

"Major announcement!" read the headline on the *Virginia Right!* website, dedicated to presenting "an unapologetic and conservative view of Richmond and surrounding areas": "Dr. David Brat to Challenge Eric Cantor in Republican Primary." The accompanying story reflected the enthusiasm of many local activists: "Brat's entry into the fray is a strong statement about the ineffectiveness of Eric Cantor during his political career," wrote Tom White, editor of *Virginia Right!*, who would be among our campaign's key promoters:

> One of Cantor's best skills has been to deceive his supporters into thinking that he is actually trying to stop Obama and reel in spending and horrible legislation like Obamacare . . . . It is time to retire Cantor and place someone in the seat that actually knows economics and is above the political games that Cantor has become so adroit at playing. I have known David Brat for several years and know him to be one of the most ethical people I have ever met as well as a brilliant thinker.

But in the wider world, the news hardly caused a ripple. Dave's first formal event was two days later, at Richmond's St. John's Church, site of Patrick Henry's historic "Liberty or Death" speech, and it was not what anyone would call an auspicious launch. Exactly nine people showed up.

ZACH'S TAKE

It was 2013, the day after Thanksgiving, and having won my first House of Delegates race, I was looking for work. I was back home in

Maryland, in the middle of an alumni lacrosse game, when a call came from Dave Brat. Chris Doss had recommended me for the campaign manager's job, and Chris and I had discussed the possibility of my employment on that race in the days leading up to the holiday.

So a few days later, I drove down to Richmond to meet with him at Panera Bread. In the meeting were Dave Brat, Larry Nordvig of the Richmond Tea Party, and me. They wanted to vet me as much as I wanted to vet Dave.

The opening was great: Dave's an econ guy, I'm an econ guy, so right off the bat I asked who his favorite economist was.

He laughed and said, "Milton Friedman."

"Okay, good–you're not a Keynesian. We're in good shape."

After a little while, we began talking about the race, and they made the case that Cantor was beatable. I was really not hard to sell, because I like long shots anyway, and I was already feeling good about Dave. He had the looks and was well spoken and obviously smart, but he didn't come off as stiff. He was affable and human; he seemed like the kind of guy who can shoot the breeze and kid around about himself as well. And he looked me in the eye and talked straight.

Even without really knowing the guy, it all added up to a feeling that he had it in him to be a good retail politician.

And there was something else. While Dave was definitely a solid conservative, and the Tea Party would be his base, no one would get away with the kind of anti-Tea Party smears that had been effective in some other races. No one could easily call him a racist yahoo or label him psychotic or as fundamentally unserious. If anyone tried–even Cantor –it would boomerang.

No question in my mind: He was the right guy. Though to this day I'm not sure what was in *his* mind. Was he hiring this 22-year-old kid because he liked my credentials and how I came across, or only because no Republican political operative in his right mind would take on Eric Cantor?

When I told my family, their reaction was—well, I suppose "protective" would be one word. "Disbelieving" might be another. Or maybe "terrified." My parents sat me down and basically said: "Listen—Eric Cantor is the most powerful Republican out there. You'll never get another job." When my grandfather, who's from southwest Virginia, heard, he laughed out loud. He asked, "What are you thinking? That's *ridiculous.*" Obviously not from a place of ridicule, but from a place of love and concern, just as with my parents.

What *was* I thinking? Well, I was young and cocky—that's definitely part of it. I'm a strong-willed guy; my mind was made up. I didn't care.

But I'd also looked at numbers that I thought showed Cantor could be in trouble. He might have looked invulnerable, but his favorability numbers were lousy, his proportion of the vote in the general had been declining in each of the previous five cycles, from a high of 75.5 percent in 2004 down to 58.4 in 2012. The trends were there. The dissatisfaction was there. The votes were there . . . and across the table at Panera Bread, the candidate was there.

Obviously it would be tough. It would take immense effort, and even then everything would have to fall into place perfectly.

But who ever said things worth fighting for are *supposed* to be easy?

THREE

THE GUY CHALLENGING CANTOR

The best thing about Dave Brat as a candidate was also the worst: By both temperament and experience, the guy was about as far from a professional politician as you could get.

On the plus side, that meant there was no chance this would be the sort of campaign GOP political operatives usually run—one that assumes voters have the IQ of roadkill. Political consultants get paid millions—in some cases *literally* (see the fools who ran Mitt Romney into the ground)—tossing around empty buzzwords and phrases from a focus group of ten they think cast a magical spell: "We're fighting for the middle class." "We're the party of the big tent." "We seek consensus." "We need to prove that we can govern." The press releases they grind out are loaded with these empty cliches.

When you get right down to it, political consulting in this country today is basically a racket. To an amazing degree, it is populated by those (perhaps formerly driven by principle) who now believe in nothing except making sure the check clears.

It's the reason—okay, just *one* of the reasons—why Americans despise politics, politicians, and the political class: The people know politicians and their compatriots have contempt for *them*.

Nonetheless, win or lose, the same consultants keep getting recycled. Look at Corey Bliss, who ran Linda McMahon's 2012 Senate race in Connecticut straight to defeat. Right before that, he ran a race up in Vermont where his candidate was up by 20 points—and he managed to blow it. Right after, in 2013, he was the consultant for a pair of winnable Virginia races and lost both. Next he worked for a candidate in the 2014 GOP Senate primary in Georgia and, after losing that, ended up in Kansas, helping run Pat Roberts's campaign. Finally, a winner—but only thanks to a major last-minute infusion of cash from outside the state, aimed at ensuring GOP control of the Senate, that dragged Roberts's tired old moderate behind across the finish line.

Does such a record give other GOP candidates pause about hiring the architect of these mutiple disasters? *Au contraire!* According to the *Wall Street Journal*, there was ferocious competition among Republican candidates in the 2016 cycle to land the services of "top consultant" Corey Bliss. (The lucky winner was Ohio Senator Rob Portman, in case anyone's looking to make some money betting on a supposed shoo-in likely to be out of work soon.)

Meanwhile, the left has largely cast off the consulting class in favor of data-driven analysts, behavioral psychologists, and tech gurus who, instead of relying on anecdotes from races in the 1970s to inform their political judgment, use science, psychology, and data. Small wonder we conservatives are so far behind.

Needless to say, Cantor's longtime consultant, Ray Allen, was of that old school of Republican consultants. In the contempt-for-voters sweepstakes, Allen has few peers. His philosophy on the Republican Party has been quoted as this: "Keep it small; keep it all."

Allen's technique relies on two basic elements: lying about his clients and lying about his clients' opponents. He is not subtle, but over the years he has been highly effective, raking in millions practicing the political black arts of obfuscation and smear. Indeed, in 2013, Allen's company, Creative Direct, was the largest single recipient of payments from the Republican Party of Virginia, to the tune of a cool $1.13 million.

Talk about a perfect match for his candidate!

On our side, with Dave Brat as the candidate, there would be none of that. Dave is a total straight shooter. He can be counted on to say the same thing in private as on the stump, and he wasn't about to be massaged or managed into something else. If anything, accustomed to having a captive audience of students, he was apt to be too policy-heavy and wonkish in his speeches and media appearances.

So what was his downside as a candidate?

The term "micro-manager" comes to mind—as in *extreme* micromanager. In his life as an academic, the trait had never been a problem. To the contrary, doing things on his own, in his own way, had served him well, not only in the classroom—where Professor Brat was accustomed to being deferred to without question—but also in the Randolph–Macon faculty lounge, where, like at almost every college these days, liberal orthodoxies rule. Indeed, had he *not* been sure of himself, and maybe a little cocky, no way he'd have dared make this run in the first place.

So it's understandable that it went against Dave's nature to do the one thing every successful candidate *must* do: delegate.

But a functional campaign can't be a one-man band, not even when the guy playing all the instruments is the candidate. It involves many moving parts working together. It means putting the right people in place and trusting them to do their jobs.

Dave sometimes referred to himself as "the campaign's CEO," which, had there been a flow chart, he certainly was. The problem, at least at the beginning, was that beneath him on the chart, there was chaos. Before announcing, he had hired a number of advisors and consultants on his own. Some were competent; some less so. But it almost didn't matter, since once the campaign was formally underway, there was little coordination among any of us. Everyone went through the candidate, and—because crucial information tended not to get shared—we were often operating at cross purposes. Dave was less a marionette than a ringmaster: If you said, "Hey, Dave—let's do this," he'd usually say, "Okay, sure—go ahead." But the effect was the same. With no clear division of responsibilities, no one but Dave knew the whole scope of what anyone else was doing, or even was *supposed* to be doing, and sometimes even Dave himself wasn't sure.

This would have been less the case if we'd had a campaign office where the various staffers and volunteers could get together and actually, you know, talk. But because the campaign was so strapped for cash, there was none. What we had was a virtual campaign office via email, with the candidate sometimes in charge, a consultant sometimes in charge, the senior advisor sometimes in charge, and, occasionally, the campaign manager in charge.

Looking back on it now, we can laugh—at least a little. But the truth is, early on, the Dave Brat for Congress campaign was a complete mess.

In fact, if things had gone a bit differently, some of the screw-ups might well have proven catastrophic. For instance, the campaign's first major fundraiser was scheduled for February 25, at the large Richmond home of a supporter. The hope was that the event would draw upwards of 100 people and raise $40,000 to $50,000—and, just as important, earn the campaign much-needed credibility with Richmond's well-heeled donor set and chattering class.

Then potential disaster. Ten days before the event, Kim Singhas got a 3 a.m. phone call—a real one, not like Hillary Clinton's in the campaign ad. It seemed the event's "hostess" claimed she had never given permission to use her home. In fact, she wasn't even going to be home that day; she would be in New York instead.

What went wrong? Who screwed up? Was it our fault, or the homeowner's? Who knows? And—Hillary again—at that point, what difference did it make?

Just then, with the slightest nudge in the wrong direction—if, say, the wrong reporter had put it on the wrong front page, or we'd have had to hold the shindig in a suburban Italian restaurant—the campaign could have gone to hell, becoming a minor laughingstock before it ever got rolling.

Instead, by a stroke of luck, one of Richmond's premiere locations, the Wilton House, had a cancellation. Built in 1753 as the home of the Randolphs, one of Virginia's great families, and now a museum of Virginia history, the new venue was in the same neighborhood as the historic University of Richmond and Country Club of Virginia, and it only enhanced our credibility. Even if many came only out of curiosity, wanting a look at the guy with the *cojones* to take on Cantor, it was standing room only at the Wilton House that evening, and the event was a stunning success. Dave was on his game, and people went away impressed.

Still, even then, there was a last-minute hitch, this time involving the refreshments—specifically, confusion over whether the food and beverages would be prepared and served by volunteers or if the campaign would have to shell out for a caterer, as we finally did.

Though the evening fell short of our fundraising goal, we at least began to put together something of a war chest. Plus we achieved something almost as vital—adding a fair number of signatures to the petitions needed to get Dave on the ballot.

That brings us to another big time screw-up from that period. According to state regulations, to appear on the 2014 congressional primary ballot, a candidate was required to post a filing fee of $3,480, and present 1,000 valid signatures on petitions, by March 27. This was the opposite of a high bar. Yet, incredibly, for a while there was actually a possibility we might not clear it. Why? Because this was one of those balls on which no one had been keeping an eye. While the consultant had put someone "in charge of" the grassroots, nobody had indicated who should be directing the grassroots to collect signatures. And we knew that 1,000 signatures weren't going to come close to being enough, since Eric Cantor and his machine were sure to have every signature closely examined and, if the margin were narrow enough, bring in a legion of handwriting experts usually reserved for assessing the validity of Hitler's diary and billion-dollar wills.

The campaign had to belatedly take on an operative to close the signature deal, and that, along with the signatures captured at the Wilton House, countless hours by volunteers in front of libraries and a couple of other events, saved our bacon. In the end, we got something close to 3,000 by the deadline, enough to discourage even Cantor's flunkies.

Dave's other liability as a candidate involved a quality that in normal life would be regarded as a positive: He found it almost impossible to ask for other people's money.

Politics being the opposite of real life, Rule One in the modern campaign playbook reads: "The answer is money. What's the question?"

Like it or not, dollars are a campaign's lifeblood. Without at least a minimal cash flow, there's no literature, no advertising, no office, no campaign.

In a campaign, the staff is the engine, the volunteers and activists are the fuel, and money is the oil. You can have the sweetest ride around, premium grade fuel, but if you don't put oil in that engine, you won't have a racecar for long.

The Seventh is a sprawling district, comprising parts of no fewer than *nine* counties and a portion of Richmond. For better or worse, Eric Cantor was known in every corner of it. Dave Brat? He was a household name in his neighborhood, some business and academic circles, and a smattering of Tea Party households. Already we were the longest of long shots; few voters knew there even *was* a campaign, and among those who did, our man was usually known only as *the guy challenging Cantor.*

Dave certainly had a compelling personal story to tell—if only we could get it out there. Son of a family doctor in rural Michigan, and brother of a professor of neuropathology at Emory (which lent weight to Dave's staunch stand against Obamacare), as a child he served as his father's "answering machine," he'd later tell *Richmond* magazine, in a family that "pushed education, hard work, integrity, doing the right thing, trying to aim your life at something that would serve others." And, indeed, before becoming a professor, he attended Princeton Theological Seminary and earned a master's degree in divinity—making it as logical as it was unusual that he taught both economics and ethics, seeing the two as inextricably linked. Add to that an attractive wife, Laura, and a pair of winning children, and you've got an unusually appealing guy as your candidate.

Sophia, Dave, Jonathan, and Laura   *Curt Deimer*

The problem was letting people know it.

Again, the ease with which even most politicians not named Eric Cantor are able to pick up a phone and ask for handouts is yet *another* reason to despise the entire breed. Dumb as politicians think we are, we're not quite dumb enough to not see that, when the "contribution" is large enough, the donor usually expects full value in return.

Still, our campaign needed cash. Needed it desperately, the way flowers need rain and sun and other politicians need cheap applause. Yet our candidate hesitated to ask even those so eager to see Eric Cantor banished from public life that they *wanted* to give. Before every appearance, whether in a church, a community center, or someone's living room, Dave would be reminded, "Ask for money. *Please* ask for money. Ask for $10 checks—$20 checks. This is a small-dollar campaign. People *want* to help." But rather than make such a direct pitch, he'd usually make a lame joke: "Hey, if you have a rich uncle somewhere, tell *him* to write a big check."

Was it possible for a candidate to be *too* ethical? This was the proof, and it drove us insane.

While Dave was an extreme case, this is a problem—and a dilemma—for other Tea Party and grassroots candidates also. Having gotten involved largely to fight the money in politics, disgusted by the influence of lobbyists and the hack pols with their noses in the public trough, it comes as a shock for them to realize that without plenty of cash, it's almost impossible to beat the jerks. Obviously, grassroots candidates must learn to overcome their squeamishness in this regard. Cashing a check doesn't compromise anyone's integrity unless that money is buying something.

Still, it was already clear the money issue would be with us until the end—as indeed it was.

Yet it is a measure of where things stood that even the funding question was overshadowed by the campaign's chronic disarray. Of particular concern was its effect on the volunteers. They were the very heart of the campaign, the ones who would have to carry the message to every part of the district if we were to have any shot at all. For many Seventh District conservative activists, too long familiar with

Eric Cantor and his methods, this was as much their fight as Dave Brat's, and from day one they'd been ready to put their hearts and souls into it. They asked little in return beyond an occasional word of acknowledgement. Yet, too often, even that ball was being dropped.

Over and over we heard that about the volunteers' frustration, and the many ways the campaign wasn't being responsive to their needs. It was a constant effort just keeping some of them on board. As one typically disheartened supporter emailed the campaign in mid-March:

> I've collected signatures, got Dave to the annual Meeting of the Cavalier Club (which led to an invitation to their spring picnic), sent emails to Walter Williams and Lou Dobbs, shared their posts with all my Facebook contacts, and just made a donation. Yet, despite two promises to add me to the [campaign's] email list, I still have to hear about things happening in the campaign second and third hand. And, I have never gotten an email thanking me for anything. It is hard to support someone when you are cut out of communications. Yes, I am frustrated. Twice I have been promised I would be added to the list.

No one was more disturbed by the campaign's often cavalier attitude toward the volunteers than Kim Singhas, who, along with Dale Taylor, ran the volunteer effort in Hanover County. Highly skilled and intensely dedicated—Laura Brat would in due course dub Singhas her husband's "campaign wife"—it was Kim who finally took it upon herself to confront Dave. They met at the Twin Hickory Library in Glen Allen, Dave's neighborhood, along with one of the campaign's redundant "consultants." "We were in one of those private study rooms," she recalls, "and I'm pounding the desk, saying 'Dave—you need a bricks and mortar campaign office to demonstrate to the voters we have a real campaign operation. They need a place to come and volunteer—make phone calls, pick up yard signs, and you need a volunteer coordinator to run it. We're less than ninety days out, we've got to get it together!'"

Dave looked momentarily shaken, then nodded. "You're right."

It was an early turning point.

ZACH'S TAKE

Not having an office in those early days was a nightmare. No desks or computers or filing cabinets! Everything was improvisation.

Though I was nominally the campaign manager, I was by far the youngest person on the campaign—Gray hadn't yet come aboard—and I spent a lot of my time on menial things, doing Dave's schedule or writing thank-you notes, and I was working out of Panera Bread and Starbucks. I'd start in the early morning at one Panera Bread or Starbucks and then, when they kicked me off the wireless, move to another. I pretty quickly learned which venues were more welcoming and which would only let you use their connection for an hour and a half and where the best public hotspots were and the places where you got lousy reception.

This was basically how it went through January, February and into March. Then there was a point where I was literally trying to run key parts of the campaign out of my little black Ford Ranger truck. I also had my two guitars in there, a Les Paul and a Fender, and the outside was plastered with bumper stickers for various polititians and bands. It had a Ron Paul and a Barry Goldwater, a big orange one that says, "Guns Save Lives," a

"Resistance to Tyrants Is Obedience to God," and one with the Virginia Citizens Defense League logo. Then on one window I had stickers for the Allman Brothers, Marshall Tucker Band, Charlie Daniels Band, and Lynyrd Skynyrd–plus one for Warren Zevon. And, of course, I had a bunch of Dave Brat stickers.

A '70s Southern rock aficionado's ride? Yes. A campaign office? Absolutely not.

It's really just a little piece of junk of a truck–but, boy, can it move! And it did a heck of a job during that campaign, and still does. I only had a major issue once, when my clutch went out on the coldest day of the year. By the end of the race, some people had even given it a name: "The Millennium Falcon of Virginia Politics."

GRAY'S TAKE

I didn't officially join the campaign until March 22. Up to that point, I'd just been following it from a distance--obviously with great curiosity.

When I first heard someone was challenging Cantor, my reaction was: "Oh, boy--he'd better be *really* good." Because I just didn't believe Cantor was beatable. Having worked for him, I knew who and what he was--and how ruthless.

At that point, in early January, I was actually thinking of leaving politics altogether. I'd come off of a very grueling, discouraging campaign the previous fall, and wasn't sure there was a future in it. The candidate was E. W. Jackson, a black minister and bedrock conservative running as the Republican candidate for Virginia lieutenant governor. E. W. was a great person, a Harvard Law School graduate with a compelling life story. But short of a perfectly run campaign, he was dead on arrival, because in his role as a minister, he'd left behind a trail of radio interviews passionately laying into the culture's abandonment of traditional Christian teaching on homosexuality. Nor was he shy about saying out loud that, as a matter of record, Planned Parenthood had killed more blacks than the KKK. Does it even have to be said that, when it comes to slavery and the KKK, the media is even more eager to take conservatives out of context than usual? Or that they have a particular scorn for *black* conservatives?

In short, passionate as I was about getting him elected, he was a long-shot candidate. It didn't matter that he was absolutely right--especially in his take on the devastating effects of liberal policy on the black family. His tone and language made his message far too easy for the other side to dismiss. And unfortunately, he chose to surround himself with yes-men who refused to take the steps necessary to counteract his negatives.

So I was really considering all options. I was doing some work for a local Charlottesville radio station, and there was a possibility of a health-care consulting job, or possibly a paralegal position down in Houston. I was also looking into the wine industry and had had a couple of interviews with wine importers.

Then, in early March, I went to a fundraiser for Dave Brat at someone's home in Charlottesville, heard him speak, and was very impressed. He was a little academic, especially compared to the usual politician, but I liked that–it was straight, no BS. It was exactly the tone that was going to be needed to defeat Cantor. Afterward, I talked to him and asked a few questions. The lesson I'd learned–which, when you're young and naive, is not as obvious as it seems–is that you'd better have a really good candidate. And on the basis of that evening, long as the odds were, I believed that maybe–possibly–if everything broke just right, Dave had it in him to win.

So I sat down and wrote him an email making the case for myself, and I included a memo outlining the direction I thought the campaign should take (see p. 204) and the pitfalls to avoid. Other people also contacted him on my behalf, including Donald Woodsmall, who had served as a senior advisor on the Jackson campaign, who wrote:

> [W]hile Gray had field responsibilities, which he was very good at, his real value is in a strategist, communicator, advisor, or press secretary type of role. He will work 18 hours a day for you and that is not hyperbole. He is a constitutional conservative and a political junkie, but he is also very sophisticated and smooth. He understands

the political game and what it takes to get elected . . . . He was impressed with you, Dave, and while he realizes he is risking something with his conservative colleagues by working against Cantor, he was impressed enough with you to risk it. I could not recommend him more highly. You should hire him if you have a position where he would fit as you won't find anybody better.

With a letter like that, how could I miss?

A couple of days later, Dave called. His manner was friendly but abrupt: "Look," he said, "I want you to help take the campaign national. So just start working–start emailing. Gotta go."

No exaggeration–it really was that brief and vague.

That's the basis on which I joined the Brat campaign, without any real direction or defined role–or even a set salary, which was kind of disconcerting. So I saw, from the outset, how disorganized and haphazard things seemed to be.

It didn't help when I received a note from one of our closest family friends. Though he was a longtime Cantor supporter, he was also someone for whom I'd always had great respect and whose counsel I valued enormously. It began:

> Gray, all I can say is that I am disappointed that you didn't consult me before you accepted your position and you don't understand the error in your judgment. Wisdom and judgment come with experience and from learning from your mistakes. Please keep an open mind and be willing to acknowledge and learn from your mistakes. I would put this in the mistake column . . .

FOUR

BEING RIGHT IS NOT ENOUGH

The Dave Brat For Congress headquarters opened on March 12, on Broad Street in Glen Allen. From the outside, it indeed projected a greater sense of professionalism.

But what is it they say about appearances and deception? Not only did the brick and mortar fail to address the underlying issues besetting the campaign, but in certain ways, it aggravated them. For it placed under the same roof a group of people who, for all their good intentions, were not meshing as a unit. Lines of communication remained confused, the chain of command was indecipherable, Dave still had trouble delegating, and assorted would-be "advisors" and "consultants" continued to jockey for position.

Obviously, conflict is a staple of every campaign. None is without its fair share of pettiness and backbiting and egos run amok. They are *all* pressure cookers.

Still, the personalities this campaign had thrown together were an especially problematic mix. Since most had activist backgrounds in common, this should have been foreseen. Indeed, what would end up being among the campaign's great selling points—its stress on individual liberty—meant it attracted people who tended to be... highly *individual,* so not necessarily good at playing well with others.

For the record, we are both grassroots Tea Party guys from way back. No movement in our lifetimes has had a greater or more positive effect on public affairs in this country than those who organized, under the banner of Taxed Enough Already, in defense of the Constitution and small government. Which is to say we have been as frustrated and royally irked as anyone over how the media and the left have slimed the Tea Party as racist, homophobic, and every other ugly pejorative that has sprung to liberal minds. In fact, the Tea Party represents the very best in the American tradition.

The Tea Party would come to mean everything to us on the Brat campaign. They were our base, and from the outset, our most passionate and steadfast supporters. We would not have come close to winning without them. Indeed, Dave was unmistakbly the Tea Party candidate in this race.

We just couldn't let him be defined that way.

Considering the odds against us, we knew we had to take to heart the lessons of the recent electoral past.

Lesson 1: Knowing we couldn't win with *only* Tea Party support, and that among the other voters we needed—libertarians, disaffected conservatives, "country club" Republicans, independents, even conservative Democrats—many would run from a "Tea Party candidate" like rats from a sinking ship. Though this was tough to swallow, since it was a product of the media's dirty work, it was political reality. The coalition we had to weave in the Seventh District was so fragile that a hard pull on any of its threads would unravel the whole thing.

Still thinking of Sir Galahad? Being right is *not* enough to win.

Which brings us to Lesson 1(a): *Never* hand the opposition (or their allies in the media) easy ammunition. This is something movement conservatives usually have found hardest to bear in mind. Long before Christine "I'm not a witch" O'Donnell, Todd "legitimate rape" Akin or Richard (pregnancy from rape) "is something that God intended to happen" Mourdock, there was Mr. Conservative himself, Barry Goldwater. We're both Goldwater fans, but his 1964 presidential campaign set the benchmark for terrible messaging. Right off the bat, in his acceptance speech at the convention, Barry made a classic unforced error when he declared: "Extremism in the defense of liberty is no vice." Sure, the base found it incredibly stirring—just watch the film of all the people in the convention hall going crazy. And for what it's worth, Goldwater was entirely correct. But simply by using the word "extremist," he gave the left a howitzer, and they pulverized him with it. From there, it was a short jump to the ad later in the campaign implying Goldwater was eager to use the nuclear bomb. Goldwater's campaign slogan was "In your heart, you know he's right." More ammunition. The Dems turned it back on him: "In your guts, you know he's nuts."

It didn't matter that it was his opponent, Lyndon Johnson, who was really the mental case, or that LBJ was already lying through his teeth about Vietnam, and well on his way to wrecking the economy (as well as wreaking havoc on the black family) with his misbegotten Great Society programs.

This is why the contrast between Goldwater's campaign and Ronald Reagan's first run in 1980 is so telling. Philosophically, the two candidates were nearly identical, yet because Reagan's campaign had its head on straight, he won in a blowout. Jimmy Carter tried to do exactly the same thing to Reagan that LBJ had pulled on Goldwater: smear him with the "radical" brush. But when Reagan responded with good humor—and refused to give liberals ammunition—it just didn't stick.

A serious campaign involves a lot more than stirring speeches at rallies and waving yard signs. It means checking one's more outspoken views—and one's ego—at the door. It means shutting up rather than risk embarrassing the candidate. It means acting and sometimes even dressing the part. It means recognizing that winning is all that matters, and presenting the candidate in the best possible light, even if that sometimes feels uncomfortably like accommodation or compromise.

And Dave got that. He knew that getting to people who'd voted for Cantor for more than a decade called for nuance, not bomb throwing. He did not want to be pigeon-holed as a Tea Party candidate, with all the baggage that carried, and he had all the attributes essential to *not* be labeled that way. To the contrary, with his clean cut looks, man-about-town style, and reassuring way of talking, Dave was a natural fit for the conservative, tradition-bound Seventh District, home to a number of the nation's founders and founding institutions.

Yet some of those helping on the campaign were his polar opposites. At times, the Brat headquarters could almost have passed as a frat house or a biker clubhouse. There were people running around in T-shirts and blue jeans, people in Birkenstocks or biker boots, and guys with tattoos and ponytails. Plus—and we're both die-hard Second Amendment supporters--there were people openly carrying.

If a reporter had gotten a look at it, we'd have been cooked.

Meanwhile, all kinds of work was still not getting done—or badly, if at all.

In a campaign as underfunded as this one, and struggling for traction, the little things take on outsized importance. If we got people into a church, or even a living room, to meet Dave, were we capturing their information so that we could follow up about volunteer work? Did everyone leave with a palm card giving the website and where to send a check? Was our signage right—large enough, properly displayed? How effective was the literature? Did it, at a glance, establish the sharp contrast between our candidate and Eric Cantor?

There was no communications director and no finance committee. Day to day, we were winging it. Though we had exalted titles—campaign manager and deputy campaign manager—as the junior guys, we were generally not regarded by the others as threatening, or even necessarily consequential. To the extent we had a job description, it was less moving the ball forward and more putting out fires.

How half-assed were things? Because the campaign had no money for desks or office equipment, volunteers from Hanover County had taken it on themselves to furnish the new office via local Goodwill and Salvation Army stores.

Within the campaign, the stresses were only growing, and things obviously couldn't continue this way.

On March 20, Dave gathered the staff in the office for what was supposed to be an air-clearing session, but it quickly turned acrimonious. All at once, everything was on the table: the complaints from the field, the lousy website, the fundraising letters full of misspellings, the crummy-looking logo on the letterhead, all the many ways this was not the professional campaign it had to be.

The most intense flashpoint was a literature piece designed by one of the consultants—this after an earlier one already had to be ditched. Dave now wouldn't approve this one, either. And he was right—it missed the mark. But as heads butted and heels dug in, it became clear that compromise was impossible.

The break came over a relatively minor issue: the campaign website. Dave hated it, and the consultant refused to change it.

All at once, the dam holding back the accumulated stress and frustration crumbled. In an instant, voices rose and recriminations flew, and over the next ten minutes it only got worse. That wasn't anyone's best moment—including ours.

Abruptly one of the consultants got to his feet. "Know what, Dave?" he said, "I'm done!" and he stalked out of the office.

A moment later, another staffer stood up, and *he* walked out as well. Then another.

Suddenly there were only three staffers left in the room—and before long the third would go on to leave the campaign as well.

On the listing ship that was the Brat for Congress campaign, we would be the last men standing.

FIVE

JUST A PAIR OF YOUNG GUYS

The task before the two of us—running the Dave Brat campaign and running Eric Cantor out of American political life—was obviously a tall order, but we welcomed it. We were young, passionate, and driven, and it is precisely challenges like this, the ones that stood to make a real difference, that had gotten us into this business.

But first we had to get to know each other.

The day the campaign blew apart, leaving us to put it back together—or, more precisely, to start it over—was little more than a week after we'd met, and in the frenzy and stress of that period, we had interacted only briefly.

But from the little we'd seen, neither of us was much impressed.

Zach: My immediate reaction on meeting Gray was: "I'm not sure I like that guy." Partly, it had to with the overall dysfunction of the campaign at that point, how things kept happening without explanation or apparent reason. Gray was one of those things. One afternoon Dave just walked into the office with Gray and announced: "This guy's joining the campaign." And the rest of us were like, "What the hell is this about?" I'd been there nearly three months, and suddenly here's this new staffer being foisted upon us with no warning and no role? Besides which, he looked about 14 years old. Seriously. I was a year younger than Gray, with wild, untamed hair and a beard, and looked like I'd been living in the mountains—and I never got carded. But when I'd later go into a bar with Gray, he'd get carded every time.

Gray: I was definitely the outsider. No one tried to hide their resentment of me, so my attitude was: "Fine, I'll do anything I can to be helpful and earn their trust." But it was really awkward, because at the same time, I could see what a mess the campaign was, and by nature, I'm very proactive. So I had a lot of ideas about what we should be doing that no one seemed to want to hear.

Zach: That was the other thing—Gray is the opposite of a shrinking violet. He's out there; he asks a lot of questions, inserting himself, sometimes over the top of you while you're speaking. And if he has an idea? Man, he lets you know what his idea is, and he will fight for it—aggressively and hard. On matters like that, I'm more laid back. I generally don't interject or interrupt unless I'm highly caffeinated or something objectionable has been said. So at first my attitude was "Screw this guy. I'm gonna make him do all the annoying, stupid crap that nobody else wants to do."

Gray: No question we're completely different kinds of people, Zach and I. He was obviously a smart guy and a skilled operative, but at that point I frankly didn't know if he'd be part of the problem or part of the solution. He grew up in rural southern Maryland—very country—and my early impression was that social niceties definitely were not his strong suit. A couple of times people came into the office who had been longtime Cantor supporters, and who might have been persuadable, but Zach's an in-your-face libertarian, and he got pretty combative. Given that we needed to run a race that would not turn off country club conservatives, I just wasn't sure about him.

Zach: So I'm piling all this drudgework on Gray, a lot of stuff that's fallen through the cracks. And within a couple of days I'm just bowled over—both by how fast he does it and by how well. I mean, he's just knocking it out of the park. We'd been looking for ways to firm up the case about Cantor's hypocrisy, and within a day or two, Gray researches all these obscure votes, explaining what each means once you get beyond the political doublespeak, and he documents it all in great detail. I was like: "Holy cow—this is just awesome!" It was the genesis of the candidate comparison that would prove so incredibly effective through the rest of the campaign.

Gray: It was immediately after the blowup that we really started bonding, as far as I was concerned. Up until then we really hadn't had all that much interaction. But now we were in total crisis mode, and everything was up in the air. Were we going to be able to get through this, or was everything going to fall apart?

In the office the next day, with the campaign in crisis mode, it was like Zach was a different guy. There was no doubt he was the real deal. He told me: "Gray, I know this isn't why you were brought on, but we need you to do field organizing. We don't have anyone else."

Of course! Absolutely!

Since we also had no lit piece, the old one being a useless piece of crap, that was another immediate priority. So Zach sat down and designed a new one, which was terrific, that we got it out in a couple of days. He turned out to be a phenomenal writer, and really, really good at policy.

There were a million other things to do to set the campaign right, but there was never a moment's doubt for either of us that we'd get them done. We leaned on each other because we had to—and our mutual respect grew very quickly.

In short, at that crucial moment, instead of being discouraged, we saw only opportunity. The campaign was a blank slate. This was our chance to start from scratch and do everything right. Messaging, press releases, radio ads, online advertising, videos, setting up events, fundraising. Everything.

Zach Werrell and Gray Delany

We ended up having our first real conversation late the night of that first day. We talked about everything—the lunacy of this campaign, our families, our different political paths that had led us to this strange place. We were just a pair of ambitious young guys, 23 and 24 years old, shooting the breeze, wondering how we came to be insane enough to take on the majority leader.

Though officially one of us was in charge and the other subordinate, that very quickly became meaningless. We worked in concert, our strengths complementary, both of us playing a role in almost every aspect of the campaign. We were about as small and lean a team as you could get, which would prove our greatest strength. We could both be certain this effort would never be derailed by ego or envy, for it was girded by our shared core passions: the country, the conservative cause, and the conviction that Eric Cantor had to be defeated in the interest of both.

Not that over the weeks and months to come there wouldn't be occasional disagreements about strategy or spending priorities, or even the odd emotional outburst brought on by stress or lack of sleep—a dozen cups of double lattes or jet black double-brews daily aren't exactly an antidote for frazzled nerves. But the storms always passed quickly.

There was no question our bond was strengthened by the fact that others—including, at times, our candidate—were so conscious of our age. While for us it was a non-issue, our youth left us far more open to second-guessing than had we been older. As terrific a candidate as Dave would prove to be, he was even more a novice in this area than we were, unused to the stresses of the campaign's daily ups and downs. And though we generally got on well, it's also fair to say he never got completely used to the fact that his fate was largely in the hands of a couple of guys who in his other life might have been anxiously awaiting his verdict on their midterms; that we were fellow professionals who had strong ideas about how things should be done, and even when he disagreed, didn't hesitate to express them. And that sometimes we might be right and he wrong.

Tactically, the two of us were on exactly the same page. We had calculated, each on his own, that if this upset were to be pulled off, two things needed to happen on June 10, and each would take a Herculean effort. (1) We would have to sledgehammer off a massive chunk of Cantor's habitual vote—around 30 percent. In other words, we'd have to convince a great many of his voters they had made a mistake every time they had voted for him over the past ten years. At the same time, (2) we would have to energize a significant number of others who previously hadn't bothered to vote at all—fed-up conservatives who generally skipped primaries in the (not unreasonable) belief their votes didn't matter.

What did that mean in numerical terms? Two years before, approximately 45,000 had voted in the primary that re-nominated Cantor. Our hope—most would have called it a fantasy—was to increase that number dramatically while at the same time reducing Cantor's total by 30 percent. Undermining the institution that was Majority Leader Cantor in his home district would be no picnic.

If, from the outside, neither one of those eventualities appeared likely (and, in fact, seemed contradictory, since they involved appeals to wholly different constituencies), within a couple of days of our partnership, a piece of news came that at least set us on the right track.

Over the previous few months, there had been growing concern about Pete Greenwald, who, after first pledging he would drop out if a more credible candidate came along—and Dave Brat was nothing if not that—had stayed in the race, aggressively pursuing signatures. Since he had no shot, there was no logical reason he was still in the race.

Our feelings, to a point, were summed up by one of our key supporters, Tom White, in a March 4 posting in his widely read web site, *Virginia Right!*:

> Peter Greenwald, I believe, is a good man. But there is no way on this earth that he is even remotely qualified let alone capable of being a U.S. Congressman. He is a complete political neophyte and his MTP [Mechanicsville TEA Party] appearance proved it. The people in attendance were looking for answers to hard questions.
>
> "How will you counter the Eric Cantor machine?"
>
> He had no clue.
>
> "It will take hundreds of thousands of dollars at least to counter Cantor's millions. What organization do you have in place to gather such financial support?"
>
> He had no answer. Maybe God. . . With all due respect, Peter Greenwald is not a viable candidate and time is just too short to pretend otherwise . . . Two challengers will ensure a victory for Eric Cantor.

Indeed, Greenwald's continued presence in the race had actually given rise to a certain paranoia, since the only plausible explanation seemed to be that he was there as a spoiler—or, to be precise, as a stalking horse for Cantor, to divide the anti-incumbent primary vote. With the deadline for filing looming, we convinced ourselves it was possible Cantor was actually bankrolling Greenwald's signature-gathering effort. In any event, it seemed a near certainty Pete would turn in the thousand signatures required by law. And while of course this did not mean he'd have a thousand *valid* signatures, there was zero chance that the Seventh District chairman who reviews those signatures, Cantor's hand-picked man, would give Pete's signatures anything but a quick once-over before declaring: "Looks to me like he has his thousand." In which case *we* might have to challenge the validity of Pete's signatures, thereby antagonizing his conservative voters, every one of whom we would eventually need on our side.

What was certain was that Cantor's machine had gone out of its way to be friendly to Pete—pointing out how he's truly a great conservative, unlike that liberal professor—and otherwise trying to draw grassroots support from Dave.

Knowing who our adversaries were and what they are capable of definitely had us on edge, and that would not change. We would continue to look over our shoulders the whole campaign.

But in this instance, we were wrong. Pete was as good as his word. At the deadline, March 27, he declined to hand in his signatures and issued this statement:

> As I end my run, based upon my deep devotion to God, family and country I recognize and endorse Dave Brat as a true conservative who must defeat Mr. Cantor. I applaud him for his efforts, and I pledge to do all that I can to help

him in his campaign. I ask you to do the same. I believe this is the best way forward to secure the blessings of liberty for generations to come.

SIX

"A *REPUBLICAN* DID ALL THAT?"

Virginia's Seventh is about as reliably conservative a Republican district as there is, so the pressing concerns of its voters in early 2014 were no mystery. Like millions of like-minded voters across the country, they were focused principally on three issues: Obamacare, our broken and lawless immigration system, and an economy built on out-of-control government spending. In short, they were for freedom and opposed to nanny-state liberalism run amok, with all its intrusive, freedom-crushing authoritarianism and growth-strangling regulation.

Obviously, it was important to effectively lay out Dave Brat's positions on these issues, establishing that he was the real deal: a man of experience and depth who had thought the issues through and reached the right (which is to say conservative) conclusions. But at least as vital was making the case that Cantor, for all his self-presentation as a "young gun" conservative and leader, was not part of the solution to the problem, he *was* the problem. He was a liar—a fraud—a purveyor of Grade-A BS.

Dave himself never put it quite that way, of course, and neither did the campaign. That wasn't who he was or what his background had prepared him for, and it was important to him that even if he lost he keep his self-respect and the respect of others. Still, he said much the same thing – just in loftier and more theoretical terms. His basic stump speech was on the Republican Creed, the six principles by which every Virginia Republican had pledged to abide, and how Cantor routinely violated the following five:

> **Principle #1: "We believe that the free enterprise system is the most productive supplier of human needs and economic justice."** Dave noted Cantor's votes for, among other measures, TARP and Fannie May and Freddie Mac, as well as how he teamed up with Steny Hoyer to increase the lending capacity of the Import–Export Bank and partnered with Maxine Waters to undo reforms to the National Flood Insurance Program.

> **Principle #2: "That all individuals are entitled to equal rights, justice and opportunities and should assume the responsibilities as citizens in a free society."** Dave dropped the A-bomb: Cantor's undermining of the STOCK Act.

> **Principle #3: "That fiscal responsibility and budgetary restraint must be exercised at all levels of govern-**

ment." What about the ten out of fourteen times that Cantor voted to increase the debt ceiling?

Principle #4: "That the federal government must preserve individual liberty by observing constitutional limitations." Cantor was a consistent supporter of government surveillance of private citizens, even voting against an amendment that would have limited wiretapping to terror suspects.

Principle #6: "That faith in God, as recognized by our founders, is essential to the moral fiber of the nation." An ethicist himself, much concerned with morality in government, Dave pointed out that during the debt ceiling fight, Cantor brought two bills to the floor simultaneously. One bill defunded Obamacare, and the other fully funded it. Though Cantor intended to pass the latter, he knew the former would help placate the grassroots. Is there a better example of double-dealing or rank immorality?

Generally, the stump speech worked. People came away impressed—both with Dave and the depth of his contrast with Cantor on the issues.

Indeed, Dave was proving to be a very good retail politician, and increasingly so as, with practice, his messaging got punchier and less theoretical. We never had the slightest concern that he'd slip up and say something the Cantor people could use to paint him as a fool or a maniac; he was always in control, never flubbed anything. Sure, sometimes he could still be guilty of paralysis by analysis, but even that could be endearing, because it was who Dave was; it wasn't put on.

Quite simply—and this is far rarer than many realize—he was his own campaign's greatest asset. When people saw him, he was an easy sell.

The problem was that the Seventh is a huge district, and he was only one human being. No matter how many church suppers, fairgrounds, and backyard barbecues we got him to, it would never be enough. It was a good bet that by the end of the campaign, only around 10 percent of those heading to the polls would be able to identify him on sight.

That's what happens in the television age when you have no money for television.

So that aspect of our job couldn't have been clearer: getting who he was and what he stood for in front of a largely indifferent electorate on the cheap, and making him the obvious and essential alternative to a nationally renowned figure able to buy all the ad time he wanted on every major media outlet from now until Primary Day.

We started by polling on the Big Three issues, seeking the precise wording that would have the greatest effect among voters in the district. These calls are not just dirt cheap, but highly effective in crafting—and perfecting—messaging.

Ron Hedlund

In general, the results of these polls were encouraging. Even when someone self-identified as a Cantor supporter, if that person stuck with the call, there proved an excellent chance that by the end he would be undecided about continuing to support Cantor—or, better yet, be pro-Dave.

It was the strongest indication to date that the first half of the Herculean lift, cooling regular Republican primary voters on Cantor, and on a large scale, was doable.

Of course, the same calls also confirmed that a certain (and fairly high) percentage of Cantor people would be beyond our reach. He was their guy, and that was that; we'd never get them even if we produced a video of Cantor french-kissing Obama. The term "Cantor Zombies" applied, and, thanks to the hilarious song *I'm an Eric Cantor Zombie* (and an accompanying video featuring a montage of zombies, including a zombie Obama and a zombie Pelosi), created by our buddy Tom White of *Virginia Right!*, among Brat supporters it soon became ubiquitous. The refrain is especially catchy:

He's a 14-trillion-dollar epic fail.

And, yes, I know his vote's for sale.

But I'll sell my soul and vote for him

And swear I won't get fooled again.

I'm an Eric Cantor zombie.

Though our website and literature featured Dave's stances on a range of issues, from guns (pro; check), to life (pro; check) to tort reform (pro; check), we always made sure to keep the Big Three issues front and center.

By far our most effective literature piece in this regard was the "compare and contrast" sheet we gave volunteers going door to door and handed out to voters at events. It bore no campaign logo, nor anything else to suggest it was anything other than strictly factual (as it indeed was), and we made copies available to anyone who was doubtful or argumentative or who just wanted to ruminate further in the privacy of home. The message was simple: "Compare the candidates; make an informed decision." So was the unspoken part: How could anyone read this and *not* want to vote for Brat over Cantor?

	DAVE BRAT	ERIC CANTOR
Debt Limit	Dave, as an economist, believes that addressing our national debt is a top priority. Dave is committed to real spending cuts in the near term and to reducing the debt burden on our future generations.	Since Congressman Cantor was elected in 2001, he has voted to raise the debt limit nine times. He also voted for the Ryan–Murray budget, which eliminated the spending caps imposed by the sequester. They were the only spending cuts Republicans achieved in the last five years (CRS Report 10/15/13).
Crony Capitalism	Dave believes that crony capitalism is eroding the public's trust in government. Dave will vote against bills that benefit big business over small business. Washington should not be in the field of picking winners and losers.	Eric added an amendment to the bipartisan STOCK Act that allowed family members to continue to inside trade (S. 2038, 2/9/12). Eric voted to bail out the big Wall Street banks in 2008 (H.R. 1424, 10/3/08). It is no coincidence that the same banks that received TARP bailout funds are also some of Cantor's largest donors.
Illegal Immigration	Dave believes that we need to secure the border before addressing immigration reform. Dave does not support amnesty.	Eric was the chief architect behind the "Kids Act," which would have provided amnesty to all illegal immigrants under the age of 30. Cantor cited immigration reform as a "top priority" in 2014.

Size of Government	Dave understands that the federal government has a spending problem, not a revenue problem. He will advocate for conservative reform that will empower people, not government.	Eric Cantor has been a consistent supporter of big government. He voted for Medicare Part D (H.R. #1, 11/22/03) and the farm bill (H.R. 2642) and voted to undo reforms to the National Flood Insurance Program (H.R. 3370, 3/4/14).
Obamacare	Dave will not vote for a bill that fully funds Obamacare. He will fight to repeal Obamacare and replace it with a free market solution that will improve access to care and lower health care costs.	Eric Cantor voted to fully fund Obamacare (H.R. 2775, 10/16/13). He has not accomplished any meaningful reforms to a law that has little public support, although he has scheduled over forty meaningless procedural votes so that House members could pretend to be on the record opposing Obamacare.
Government Surveillance	Dave believes that the Constitution does not need to be compromised for matters of national security. He supports the end of bulk phone and email data collection by the NSA, IRS, or any other branch of government.	Eric voted for the National Defense and Authorization Act (H.R. 1960, 6/14/13), which authorizes the unconstitutional bulk data collection by the government under the PRISM program. Eric voted against an amendment offered by Justin Amash that would have allowed the NSA to collect phone records on only those that are terror suspects (H.R. 2397 Amendment 70).

We were soon getting reports of how often, after reading the material on Cantor, voters expressed surprise, indignation or even anger. They said things like "C'mon, that couldn't be true!" or "Really, a *Republican* did all that?" or "Really, Eric Cantor?!!" It may not have been news that Congress and big business play by a different set of rules than ordinary people, but that this corruption and cronyism was epitomized by their own congressman—the House majority leader, no less—how shocking!

The power of our populist/libertarian/conservative message was beyond question. Yes, We the People are getting screwed by these jerks. And, yes, if we let them, they'll keep on doing it. But, yes, we *can* fight back.

Here is the candidate and now is the time!

ZACH'S TAKE

This job was all-consuming, obviously. Even if there'd been ten of each of us, that wouldn't have been enough.

But in a way, that made it a perfect fit for me. I don't have a wife. I don't have a mortgage. I don't even have a dog. I just had this job.

I was staying part-time at Chris Doss's house, but a lot of nights I'd sleep on a cot in the office. Then the cot ripped, which was devastating, so it was the floor. But I didn't mind. Sleep was a chore, an annoyance; it got in the way of everything that had to be done. At night I would think, "God, do I have to sleep *again*? Okay, fine–I'll sleep." But once I turned out the light, I'd sleep like a lead balloon. And it was very convenient. I didn't have to take a shower or drive–I'd wake up and already be at work! How many of Cantor's people could say that?

Socially, my life was pretty much dead, unless you consider rolling into the local Irish pub twenty minutes before closing time to order a beer a social life. At least the attractive bartender got to know me–by sight.

It's not like my role in the campaign enhanced my status with women: I'm not sure if there were any groupies around the campaign, but if there were, none was within fifty years of my age.

Telling a woman you've bravely stood up to some small-minded liberal reporter just doesn't work as a pickup line. Believe me—I've tried.

SEVEN

"WHO AMONG YOU IS WITH ME?"

From the very beginning to the campaign's final day, our chief focus was on the volunteer effort: recruiting, training, and equipping an ever-growing army to carry the message block by block, living room to living room.

The volunteers were the campaign's heart and soul. They were everything, the indispensable resource, the lifeblood. It was only their belief in the effort that made victory even remotely plausible. So keeping the volunteers energized and confident was essential.

This is why it was such an immense stroke of luck, truly a game-changer, that Kim Singhas, who was running the volunteer effort in Hanover County, had been in the office on the afternoon of the blow-up. As things escalated, with voices rising, it suddenly hit her that several volunteers were due at any moment to work the phones.

Dashing from the room, she locked the front door. Anyone who tried to enter was told that the office was closed for an important meeting.

"I mean, we had World War III going on back there," she recalls. "You can't have people walking in hearing those who are supposed to be in charge screaming at each other like banshees."

Especially not in this campaign—one so driven by idealism, selflessness, and hope. You couldn't pay people enough to do what our volunteers were doing for nothing. Ask Eric Cantor.

If word had gotten out what was going on behind the scenes, the fallout could have been nothing short of catastrophic.

Psychology is an important element in any campaign, but never more so than in an underfunded grassroots effort easily cast as quixotic, even foolhardy. So widespread was the assumption that Eric Cantor could never be beaten that to many, even trying seemed pointless; and that's before you got to the widespread feeling that getting publicly known in the Seventh District as having crossed Eric Cantor could be, let us say, problematic in other respects. It might give pause to a small businessperson who had to deal with government regulators, for instance, or even someone in the country club set considering hosting an event for Dave.

So in our volunteer recruitment efforts, it was vital to establish, first and foremost, beyond all question, that no matter what people had heard, the Brat campaign was *serious*.

This began with our volunteer recruitment form. Where a campaign typically uses an Excel spreadsheet to capture a potential volunteer's name, number and email address, ours asked questions— *Will you make phone calls? Will you email? Will you knock doors? Will you work the polls?*—that enabled us to prioritize. We always followed up first with those who checked "door-knock," because they were more likely to be dedicated.

And followed up *quickly*—usually within twenty-four hours, leaving almost no lapse between people thinking they might do something and actually getting them involved.

Obviously, you couldn't just give new volunteers a walk list and send them out to the doors. So the first time generally doubled as a training exercise. After talking with a new volunteer and establishing the beginnings of a relationship, we went out with them and showed them how it's done.

The approach at the door was pretty basic: briefly establish rapport with the voter, then move on to the three central issues: Obamacare, illegal immigration, and the debt limit or the national debt. Then came the compare-and-contrast part of the conversation. Usually, there were two things prospective voters did not know—how Cantor had voted on any of those issues and much of anything about the guy running against him. No surprise there. Dave Brat? Heck, millions of Americans couldn't even tell you who the vice president is.

Though this might not be a problem for the likes of Joe Biden (to the contrary, Democrats *like* their voters ignorant), it was a hurdle we had to overcome, and we advised always starting with the information—likely to impress—that Dave was an economist. The more informed a voter, the better for us; it was the Cantor zombies who metaphorically closed their eyes, put their hands over their ears and repeated, "I can't *hear* you!"

The immovable Cantor supporters were few and far between. Most voters, having heard the pitch, pronounced themselves at least undecided. No one would actually admit "Hey, the country may be going down the tubes, and I know Cantor is part of the problem, but as long as my portfolio is going up 20 percent a year, I can't vote for change." Because at that point, the only real justification for supporting Cantor would be enthusiasm for the economic policies he supported—starting with the Federal Reserve's artificial inflation of the stock market; i.e., policies that were leading the nation to ruin.

Every interaction with a voter was unique, of course—there are as many ways to describe Cantor's duplicitous RINO behavior as Eskimos have words for snow—but this was the basic formula with which volunteers went out.

It need hardly be said that volunteers come in all shapes, sizes, and psychological permutations, and along with the dedicated worker bees were some washouts, people who made extravagant promises but never showed up, and other people who showed up just to treat the office like a social club. But there were far, far fewer of these than in most campaigns. Generally, our people cared deeply about this cause.

Beyond the obvious—passion and ease with people—what qualities made effective volunteers? Number one was smarts. Because we wanted informed voters, it was essential that those engaging them have a full grasp of the issues. We could not send somebody out as an emissary of the campaign under-gunned. Plenty of voters, too, had their own strong views, and plenty more enjoyed arguing with our volunteers just for the hell of it. This was not a task for the faint-hearted, or the ignorant.

It's probably not surprising that so many of our volunteers were older, in their late fifties, sixties, or seventies—old enough to be our parents and grandparents. Knowing the country as it had been, they were especially alarmed at where it was and where it seemed to be going. For some, the race was about defeating Cantor; for others, it was about electing Dave Brat. But for all of them, it was about refusing to give up on the future.

Our volunteer recruitment efforts were somewhat hampered by the fact that some local GOP units were effectively arms of the Cantor campaign, so we had no access to their membership lists. But on the plus side, there were multiple Tea Party organizations in the district, on whom we could count for scores of dedicated volunteers, many battle-tested from earlier campaigns.

The 63 percent of the vote that we ended up receiving in Hanover County was no accident. The event that laid the groundwork for our eventual victory was a town hall on April 10th. Organized by the Hanover Friends of Dave Brat, it was held at Life Church, a 500-seat venue with amphitheater seating. Though Dave taught at Hanover County's Randolph Macon, at that point few voters—or even activists—knew much about him. Kim Singhas and her army of Hanover volunteers spent countless days making phone calls, hand-addressing event invitations, and dropping off invitations at local businesses. Travis Witt, of the Virginia Tea Party Patriots Federation, was recruited to introduce Dave. He showed up in full Revolution-ary regalia, then whipped the audience into a patriotic frenzy with a stirring address about Peter Muhlenberg, the Woodstock, Virginia, minister who in the middle of a Sunday sermon in 1776 demanded, "Who among you is with me?" and threw off his vestments to reveal that he was in uniform—the very one Witt was wearing now. The message was lost on no one—he was challenging this audience to join this fight, just as Muhlenberg had challenged his congregation to join that earlier fight for freedom. That night, we signed up more than 100 new volunteers, and the event was crucial in raising Dave's name recognition, especially in Hanover County. Kim encountered two of Cantor's largest donors as they left the church; grim-faced, they would scarcely acknowledge her. Clearly, they realized they might actually have a fight on their hands.

Among the new volunteers the meeting produced were a retired couple from Charles City County—not even in the congressional district—named Pete and Irene Churins. There would be no more fitting representatives of the entire volunteer effort.

At that point, New Kent County was a real problem. Ideally, we would have a strong organization in every one of the district's nine counties and Richmond City, but that wasn't going to happen. If we had the other side's resources, we'd also have loved to take every identifiable Republican in the Seventh District out for dinner and personally drive to the polls every one on whose vote we knew we could count. But because we had to prioritize scarce resources, we were forced to focus on the more populous counties and higher-value precincts. In Hanover, we seemed to be in good shape—Kim and the rest of the Hanover crew had things under control—so we were putting as many volunteers as possible into the other densely populated counties of Henrico and Chesterfield. But we had almost nothing going on in some of the smaller rural counties, among them New Kent. We were way behind there.

Enter the Churins. They were so impressed with Dave at the Life Church event they decided to fully devote themselves to the campaign.

Pete was a no-BS retired Navy fighter pilot and intelligence officer, and he and Irene soon proved to be on a mission.

"Oh yeah," he says, "we were in our element. I figured we were outnumbered ten to one, just the odds we like, and boy, those poor bastards, we were just going to rip the hell out of 'em. It got to the point [the campaign] became an obsession."

Pete and Irene, along with Matt Myer, a retired doctor from Williamsburg, organized and mapped out all of New Kent—every neighborhood, every street—knocking on doors from then until election day, refining their technique along the way.

Pete and Irene: Super door-knockers

"The idea was to make sure you got the best bang for the buck every time you knocked on a door," he recalls:

> There's a thing in sales that says he who speaks first loses. Well, after you introduced yourself, there was often this moment where they wanted to express themselves and you'd just listen. That's how you made the connection. If someone had been in the military, we talked about the military, if they wanted to talk amnesty, we talked about that. The constant was that people were worried, and

angry; they'd say, "[When] I look at my country, I see it being destroyed." Here they went out and worked hard every day and they were getting played by the system. I'd tell them, "If you want a change, you want to get out there and vote. Because Dave Brat needs your help."

Pete and Irene's grasp of the issues was absolute, and in case prospective voters wanted to further research things on their own, they'd have prewritten addresses for pertinent websites on the back of the Cantor–Brat comparison sheet.

Still, as effective as anything else was their very example: "Just like we could read them, people could read us. You know, they'd see these senior citizens walking down their street in 90-degree weather, talking up this no-name professor, and that meant something. Because they could see how much we believed in Dave."

"You know," he adds, "sometimes someone would say, 'What makes you so sure Dave won't turn into a RINO?' And I'd say, 'Look, I'm a fairly good judge of character. I like this guy; I'm out here pounding the pavement for him, and I would be surprised if he did that. But if he did, then know what? I'd work to get rid of him.'"

By the end of the campaign, they'd shelled out more than $800 for gas out of their own pockets, and their farm was suffering from neglect. But we won New Kent with 63 percent of the vote, second only to Hanover as Dave's best county.

These two, with Matt Myer and a handful of others, delivered an entire county. Volunteers like this are the story of this entire campaign in microcosm.

EIGHT

CANTOR VS. THE HENRICO TEA PARTY

Eric Cantor's campaign strategy was not complicated.

Publicly, he pretended Dave Brat did not exist. Privately, he and his people went after anyone who did otherwise; with those foolish enough to actually support Dave informed they could expect the political equivalent of a shiv to the gut.

This applied even—maybe especially—to members of the media.

It took a while for us to completely grasp this. After all, a challenge to the powerful House majority leader from the right seemed a terrific story that fit right into their narrative of a GOP civil war, especially with the national political media based just 100 miles up I-95, in Washington. Moreover, since at the time a similar race pitting Tea Party challenger Matt Bevin against would-be Senate Majority Leader Mitch McConnell in Kentucky was already receiving major national play, it seemed a gimme that the media, dull-witted as they can be, would link the two.

Though such coverage surely would not be positive—we weren't *that* naive—it could only help our languishing fundraising efforts and elevate Dave's name ID.

Yeah, right. Fat chance.

From the start, the media narrative on the race might as well have been scripted by Ray Allen, Cantor's lead consultant: "The Brat campaign is a lost cause. Nothing to see here, folks. Move along." And if it wasn't actually scripted, it came pretty close, for behind the scenes, Cantor's people were working to both sustain the narrative and *enforce* it. This was done in the usual way those in power generally deal with the lapdog media, the message none too subtly conveyed that those who broke ranks would be frozen out.

As a result, right until the evening of his stunning victory, the coverage of Dave Brat and his campaign in the mainstream national press was limited to exactly two pieces: A *National Review Online* story at the start of the race that was very fair to us and a piece in left-leaning *Politico* three months later that basically took the approved line, noting that Brat has "just $40,000 in the bank" and has "little chance of upsetting Cantor in the June 10 primary." No matter. In both cases, Cantor's people reacted with outrage. They called the *NRO* reporter's editors, making her life miserable, and the *Politico* reporter got personally raked over the coals by Cantor *consigliere* Ray Allen.

Ray Allen: Always in the background *Curt Deimer*

They didn't care about tone or content. What they wanted was a total blackout.

The pressure on the local media was, if anything, even more intense. Given the Cantor angle and the district's proximity to the nation's capital, the *Washington Post* counted as local, and its Jenna Portnoy did run a few fair articles. But the *Post*'s readership was not the conservative base we needed to reach—and *that's* who the Cantor machine was determined to keep us from reaching. Indeed, looking back, the handful of radio hosts who had Dave on their broadcasts, and especially those who did so repeatedly—like John Fredericks, Doc Thompson on the *Blaze*, and local hosts Rob Schilling and Joe Thomas out of Charlottesville—stand out as profiles in courage. After Dave's first appearance on Fredericks's popular syndicated show, the host immediately received a not-so-veiled threat from Cantor's chief of staff: "John, we've been very good to you over the years. If you have Dave Brat on your show one more time, we're never coming on again." Fredericks had Dave back on the next day.

But those were very much the exceptions. Day after day, week after week, we tried to get Dave booked on other outlets heard in the district, and we were continually brushed off, even by those hosts and producers with whom we had strong relationships dating back to earlier campaigns. Many had information—guess who from— that internal polling showed Dave would lose in a landslide and be lucky to break 30 percent. So, we'd get, "We'll get back to you if the race gets closer." Those were the nicer ones. Many didn't bother to return our calls at all.

The same strong-arm tactics were being applied to potential donors, who were hearing from Ray Allen that there would be "consequences" if they gave to Brat. There was no need to spell out the particulars. Cantor had the means to exact payback—through regulatory action or the targeted removal of tax breaks, on top of local political and social consequences—and no one doubted he would. This was a guy, like Obama, for whom the usual checks on authority didn't apply when it came to perceived enemies.

So we often heard, even from those we knew to be in our corner, "I'd love to, but you have to show me some polling." Or: "Sorry, but I just don't think you can win."

But, once again, there were heartening exceptions to the mealy-mouthed rule. For instance, there was the longtime sheriff of Hanover County, an old Cantor friend. After his name was listed as a sponsor of a Brat fundraiser, he received a personal call from Cantor asking him to stop by the office. When he arrived, Cantor demanded to know "what the hell" he thought he was doing. "Congressman Cantor," he replied, "you're not the same person I knew. When I learned what you did with the STOCK Act, I knew that there was no way that I could ever vote for you again." And he walked out of Cantor's office.

But in general, the systematic marginalization had exactly the effect that Cantor's people wanted it to: It was demoralizing, especially to our troops. Indeed, such a narrative was self-fulfilling, the deafening silence about the Brat campaign confirming the sense that there scarcely *was* a Brat campaign. And without the resources to answer back, trying to counter it was shouting into a wind tunnel.

Under the circumstances, the reluctance on the part of so many to identify themselves with us, though certainly cowardly, was also understandable. Approaching the midway point in the campaign, Cantor's internal numbers were probably accurate. Beyond question, we were far behind. And there was also no question that when Cantor won, there would be plenty of scores to be settled.

That's why the Henrico Mass Meeting couldn't have come at a better time. The meeting's purpose was to choose delegates to represent Henrico County at the forthcoming and much larger GOP Seventh District Convention, which would then elect the party's district leadership.

To those untutored in the ways of Virginia politics, it would surely have seemed a minor political event of only local interest. But to the Brat campaign, this Henrico Mass Meeting would be a tremendous and much-needed morale booster.

In previous years, the meeting's deliberations had usually held all the excitement of drying paint. But 2014 was different. For in response to the threat posed by the Tea Party to the Establishment wing's control of the Virginia GOP, Cantor's machine had recently resorted to tactics that were thuggish even by its own low, brass-knuckled standards. It had been systematically exploiting the rules at county mass meetings throughout the state to ensure that rivals were excluded from even participating in the process.

They did this by using an obscure parliamentary procedure known as "slating." Because Virginia does not have party registration, this procedure had been designed to exclude Democrats seeking to infiltrate Republican gatherings. Traditionally, it was invoked by the presiding officer to "slate off" only the handful in attendance who were not readily identifiable as Republicans or were otherwise deemed suspect. Historically, participants who were Republicans and had made the effort to attend were automatically designated as delegates.

But now all that had changed. Cantor's allies, who ran many of these meetings throughout the state, had already succeeded in disenfranchising the grassroots and conservative factions in multiple counties, most notably at the Virginia Beach Mass Meeting, where hundreds of conservatives had shown up to file as delegates, and every last one had been slated out by the Cantor faction, leaving only thirty-four hand-picked Cantor allies as delegates. It was as filthy and dishonest as politics gets this side of Chicago—or maybe North Korea.

Word had it that Eric Cantor's machine intended to do the same in Henrico, Cantor's home county and the largest in the Seventh District.

Cantor himself did not attend the meeting. Unwilling to debate Dave, he couldn't risk being in the same room with him, let alone sharing a platform. A photo might be snapped, and the "optics" would not be good. But his key operatives were all there—Young Guns Virginia director Michael Lowery, campaign manager Marty

Ryall, chief of staff Kristi Way, and, pulling all the strings, Ray Allen. They took it for granted that the usual combination of bullying and brisk parliamentary maneuvering would be more than enough to roll whatever opposition showed up. After all, they had everything on their side—every elected official, the entire GOP organization, and all the money necessary to buy anyone who needed to be bought.

Then again, they didn't count on the guile and organizational skills of our grassroots organizers in Henrico, Mark and Anita Hile.

The Hiles are precisely the sort of people such Establishment types don't think matter—regular people who live in a modest home in a middle class neighborhood. They don't exactly run in the same social circles as the Establishment. But the Hiles knew full well how the regular Republican county organization had been corrupted, and they'd decided to do something about it, founding the Henrico Tea Party. In the intervening years, they had painstakingly built it into a powerful force in the county.

And it all led to this moment.

When the meeting got under way, the regulars found themselves confronting a huge disciplined grassroots guerilla army with an attitude straight out of the old movie *Network*: "I'm mad as hell, and I'm not going to take it anymore!"

Our people.

A short time later, Dave was given the opportunity to speak, and as he took the floor, as the only congressional candidate present, he had the big stage to himself . . . and he was never better.

"Why am I running? Because Washington D.C. is absolutely broken," he proclaimed, to cheers. "The economy is broken . . . and that's largely because members of Congress do not understand what a free market is. There's a big difference between being pro–free market and pro–big business. My opponent Eric Cantor runs on the Chamber of Commerce and the Business Round table agenda, point after point after point. I'm running on *free* markets, which is not showing favoritism to *anyone*."

The place shook with cheers.

"Take a look at Obamacare. Who gets to exempt themselves out of Obamacare?"

Shouts of "Congress!" as Dave began ticking off on his fingers: "Congressional staffers. Big business and unions, for starters. Do *you* get exempted out of Obamacare?"

"No!"

"Would Obamacare have passed if big business were not exempted?"

"Nooo!"

"Eric Cantor was on a Sunday show a few weeks ago promoting parts of amnesty. Again, who wants amnesty? Big business! Why does big business want amnesty? Cheap labor! So big business gets cheap labor, and what do you get? The shaft!

"And who pays the unanticipated costs that come with amnesty? Food stamps, Medicare, Medicaid, who's gonna pay the tab? You!

". . . Eric Cantor voted for debt ceiling increases in 2002, 2003, 2004, 2006, and 2007. The debt is now at $17 trillion—$127 trillion in unfunded liabilities. Social Security, Medicare, Medicaid, Bush prescription drug plan. $127 *trillion*. Have you heard leadership on the Republican side or the Democrat side mention that number?"

"Nooo!"

"If you haven't heard that number, leadership is not leading. *I* will mention that number. *I'll* go to the podium, talk loudly into the mic, and share those numbers with the American people. It is not fair to the next generation. And that's just the unfunded portion of our liabilities . . . . So I'm asking for your vote. I am asking for your support. *I* will represent you and your voice!"

As he walked off to a sustained ovation, the Cantor-aligned chairman with the gavel tried desperately to regain control. When order was somewhat restored, he announced that nominations for the all-important position of temporary chair would be limited to a single candidate—their own.

But this was met by a new chorus of boos from the floor, the attendees so infuriated that Cantor's man was forced to put the anointed candidate to a vote. Incredibly, he was rejected. The position—and, with it, control of the meeting-was up for grabs. Thanks to the plan orchestrated by Russ Moulton, one of the mastermind's of the opposition organization, the Hile faction immediately put up a candidate of their own.

Over the fifteen minutes that followed, the Establishment fought like cornered animals. All around they could be seen arm-twisting and offering deals, trying to swing things their way.

All we could offer was a fair and open process—what used to be known as democracy. The vote was close—178–173—but our guy was the winner.

Around the hall, people backslapped and hugged, disbelief mingling with euphoria. For once, incredibly, the bullies had been beaten. There would be no slating of conservatives or Tea Partiers in Henrico.

Over the weeks and months to follow, we would look back on this event as a springboard for all that followed. Among other things, it brought to our campaign a vast new cadre of volunteers from outside the district, who'd long been angered by the Establishment's ugly tactics and whose fatalism had now given way to hope. More than a few would regularly drive two hours each way from Virginia Beach to knock on doors to defeat Cantor.

Above all, it was proof conclusive of something that even some already with the campaign had secretly doubted was possible: We could go toe to toe with Cantor's forces—and win.

Tellingly, there came one last test that day in Henrico. Some of our people argued that now that we were in control, it was time to feed Cantor's side a stiff dose of their own medicine and slate *them* out. And who could deny the idea had a certain appeal? But wiser heads, among them Dave's and the Hiles', quickly prevailed.

We did not slate the Establishment's delegates, and every good Republican who took the time to file as a delegate retained the right to attend the upcoming District Convention.

Slating isn't how we did things, or how we wanted to win. We hadn't come this far to behave like our enemy.

NINE

"LIBERAL PROFESSOR DAVE BRAT"

T he Mass Meeting's impact was immediate; in its wake, you could *feel* the campaign kick into a higher gear. Every grass-roots campaign builds organically, on small successes. But this was a success of a different order, both because it was so unexpected and because it was so embarrassing to the other side.

Still working his day job, Dave was doing more events now: speeches, festivals, and meet-and-greets all over the Seventh. While they attracted little notice outside the cocoon of the campaign, almost every one brought in new volunteers and much-needed cash. Not a lot—a thousand here, maybe three hundred there, sometimes a bit more—but it kept the lights on and the volunteers supplied with literature, with enough left over to put away a little something for some media on the homestretch. We'd long since stopped thinking in terms of big checks; they weren't coming.

By far the best evidence of the race's changing dynamic came from the other side. All at once, the Cantor campaign did a complete about-face. Rather than treating Dave Brat like a nonperson, a ubiquitous Cantor ad that began running in mid-April tried to turn him into a joke. The ad's premise was that Dave—or, as he was insistently referred to, "Liberal Professor Dave Brat"—was the fraud and hypocrite in the race. The proof? Back in 2006, Governor Tim Kaine, a liberal Democrat, appointed Dave to a nonpartisan economic board whose members were charged with providing a forecast of the U.S. and Virginia economies. Though the board was expressly forbidden by Virginia code to give policy advice, the Cantor campaign claimed Dave advised Kaine to raise taxes by a billion dollars, then stood idly by during Kaine's (failed) attempt to pass the then-largest tax increase in Virginia history.

"Now liberal David Brat is running for Congress as a Republican," said a reasonably voiced woman at the end of the ad. "Liberal college professor, Tim Kaine advisor, a *Republican?* Come on, professor. You've got to be kidding."

As "evidence" of Dave's liberalism, the Cantor campaign cited as its source the impressive-sounding WECHECKTHEFACTS.COM. In fact, anyone who actually bothered to check would discover that WECHECKTHEFACTS.COM was entirely a creation of the Cantor campaign—with the disclaimer "Paid for and Authorized by Cantor for Congress" right on the site.

This was Cantor tactician Ray Allen's slash-and-burn, win-at-all-costs mentality at its most appalling, taken straight from the Establishment playbook that says you spew whatever poison you think will work, give it massive play and, especially if the other guy has no resources to fight back—you'll get your way.

Aside from the rest, it showed the Cantor campaign's complete and utter contempt for the voters' intelligence.

The truth is, *"Liberal* Professor Dave Brat" was conservative to his very core; on his own campus, he was the guy who stood up to leftists. This attempt to link him to the big-government liberal policies that were destroying the country—and, worse, to the politically correct insanity running rampant on American campuses, was a classic Big Lie.

But, for Dave, the ad was even worse than that. Not only did it falsify his beliefs, it went out of its way to belittle him personally, depicting him as a cartoon figure running around spouting squeaky gibberish.

Eric Cantor's forces were sending a message. They wanted not just to beat Dave Brat, but to humiliate him—ripping him up so badly for daring to take on Eric Cantor that no one would ever have the audacity to mount a serious challenge against Cantor again.

What was worse, the endless trumpeting of the lie seemed to be having the desired effect on the voters. Volunteers in the field said people raised it often, and that even some of those who thought it was exaggerated, or campaign rhetoric, figured it must have at least *some* basis in fact. After all, they couldn't say it otherwise, could they? Cantor would not lie to them, would he?

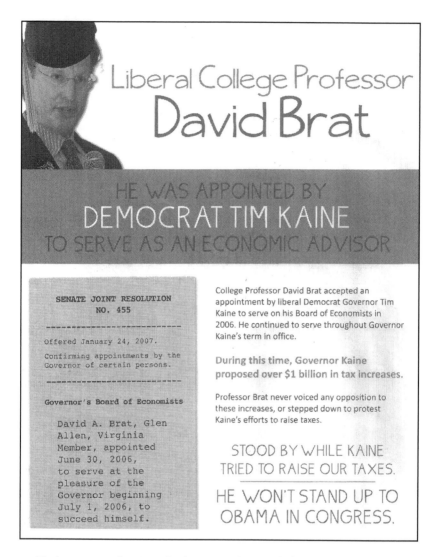

Did it get under Dave's skin? You bet it did!

Once again we looked to the local media to do their job and expose this lie for what it was. Although *Politifact* reported the ad was untruthful, the story got almost no media play. So we were again making endless calls, pleading with members of the media: "Guys, it's such an incredible lie—how can you *not* call them on it? Or even cover it?" Dave would often email reporters personally, begging them to wake up, sometimes including the article from *Politifact* as corroboration.

But the herd had its narrative, and it was Cantor the inevitable, not Cantor the mudslinging liar. That the most important newspaper in the district, the *Richmond Times-Dispatch*, would be AWOL was par for the course—Diana Cantor had recently served on the board of its parent company—but what we never expected is that *Bearing Drift*, the most widely read and influential conservative blog in the state, would seemingly be in the tank for Cantor as well. Where a newer (and, alas, less widely read) web site aimed at Virginia's conservative and libertarian grassroots, The Bull Elephant, enthusiastically reported conservative superstar Ann Coulter's having written that Dave was among the top GOP insurgents to support "if you don't think the Republican Party should speak exclusively for Wall Street, Silicon Valley and the Chamber of Commerce," *Bearing Drift* ignored the story and echoed the 'liberal professor' lie verbatim: "Liberal professor Dave Brat's campaign has been quite a circus, and he has been the tightrope act. After years as a liberal academic elitist, he now switches feet to try to attack Eric Cantor from the right . . ."

Here is a sampling of their headlines over the last two months of the campaign: "Liberal Professor David Brat Pulls a Two Face Two Step." "The Despicable Fringe." "Where's Dave?" (this regarding Dave's having skipped a meeting with taxpayer advocate Grover Norquist to attend to his work as a professor). "Where Are Brat's Disclosure Forms?" (*Bearing Drift* refused to issue a retraction when its assertion that we'd been late with Dave's financial disclosure forms was proven wrong.)

To all appearances, whenever Ray Allen needed a quick hit piece from outside the campaign, *Bearing Drift* was just a phone call away.

Quite simply, the media didn't care about the truth. There was scarcely a word challenging the "liberal professor" lie—or any of the others.

What's even more appalling was that some Dave considered personal friends wouldn't defend him, either. He practically blew a gasket on the phone with a key player in a local faith-based lobbying organization, trying to get him to speak up. "Tom," Dave pleaded, "you know he's lying about me! You work for an organization that talks about morality and faith! Well, do you believe what you say you believe or not? Do you believe what you read in the Bible?"

When Dave played the Bible card, you knew he was at wit's end. But even that didn't work. On the other end of the line, the obviously embarrassed gentleman could be heard repeating: "Dave, I like you as a person."

"That's not good enough—I need you to speak up!"

But he never did come to Dave's defense, and neither did very many others.

Dave's a proud, principled, and decent person, and the Cantor campaign's viciousness—and others' cowardly reaction to it—was not the sort of thing he'd thought he was signing up for in undertaking this campaign. Neither had his wife, Laura, a private person who was naturally protective of their kids. There was a ton of stress on them both, and it would only get worse.

Fortunately, our old friend Chris Doss had come aboard as senior consultant. Though not involved in the campaign day to day, he was a huge steadying influence, both for Dave and for us. About a week after the blow-up, he came down to Richmond from Arlington, Virginia, where he lived and worked, and took the two of us out to dinner, and we talked through the campaign. We discussed in detail what we needed to do to win, putting in place the plan that we would follow every single day until June 10. He stressed that our focus should be on getting 1,500 people to bring fifteen people apiece to the polls. *Keep your eye on the prize*, he repeatedly told us. *Don't worry about the media, the Club for Growth, the NRA, or anything else.*

After that dinner, we talked maybe three times a week. We sent him scripts for radio ads, and he tweaked press releases and fliers; we'd talk over our digital media strategy or have conference calls with Conversant Media, our ad buyers. We just didn't have certain kinds of experience, and when we were talking about a fifteen or twenty thousand dollar ad buy, we needed the advice of someone we could absolutely trust. He wasn't trying to gouge us, and he wasn't getting a kickback from anyone; he could honestly evaluate these different vendors and help us figure out who to go with and what we needed to say.

As for Dave, he definitely found it reassuring to have on the team a guy who was more or less a contemporary. In contrast, *our* relationship with our candidate remained complicated. There were times, lots of them, when we got along great, whether talking strategy as we headed to an event or just shooting the breeze. Unlike so many politicians (probably because he'd never been one), Dave had zero sense of entitlement. He could walk into a gathering without some staffer providing notes on who to talk to and what to say, and relate to anyone, from a wealthy clubwoman to a bunch of bikers belting down beers.

Still, he never got completely used to having ceded so much control to a pair of guys basically the same age as the kids he was teaching. We got that. Obviously, a certain wisdom comes with experience. You learn things along the way, as we certainly did. But it doesn't take a Karl Rove to understand an election is basically a numbers game. And that you have to stay on message and can't say stupid things. When it comes down to it, if you're not being stupid and reckless, age isn't necessarily a factor.

Of course, it didn't help that both of us were sure enough of ourselves to challenge him or question his judgment. Nothing personal, but the campaign had a million moving pieces, and all of it mattered, from the wording of every press release to how every dollar was spent. Things were happening nonstop, we were all putting in fifteen and eighteen-hour days, and sometimes tact fell between the cracks.

One of Dave's closest confidantes during the campaign, aside from his wife Laura, was another peer, Ron Hedlund, owner of AIS Industrial Services, a Richmond-based motor sales and repair business. Ron was a former chairman of the Alleghany County GOP and Governor Jim Gilmore appointee. He was mentored over twenty years ago by party stalwarts- Donald Huffman, Don Duncan, Pete Giesen, and Bob Goodlatte. But after being away from politics for several years, he decided that he had seen enough from the Cantor machine and that it was time to get involved again. Like a number of other volunteers in the campaign, Ron was taking a course from the Tennessee-based Center for Self Governance stressing how much our republic depends on individuals' exercising their civic authority with candidates, and he had put his career on hold for the duration to help out the campaign.

The Brats, Ron Hedlund, the AIS Liberty Dually

Among other things, he often drove Dave to events in his truck, a rolling patriotic tableau he'd named the AIS Liberty Dually. It was festooned on one side with the Declaration of Independence, the Bill of Rights, Mount Rushmore, quotations from the Founders and other notable aspects of the American story; on the other was a tribute to family members who'd served in the nation's armed forces; and dominating it all were huge DAVE BRAT signs standing erect in the bed of the behemoth. Over long hours on the road, Ron was Dave's sounding board, and among the frustrations and doubts to which he gave vent were a few about us.

Apparently one question came up fairly often: Can we be sure these kids know what they're doing?

Call it cockiness, but, yes, we were absolutely sure. As far as we were concerned, the campaign was right on course, its trajectory perfect.

The "liberal professor thing?" It depended how you looked at it. Of course, it was an outrage. Obviously. But would they have launched such an ugly ad blitz if after the Henrico Mass Meeting they weren't at least a little concerned? More to the point, in doing so, they'd given Dave Brat the kind of name recognition we could never in our wildest dreams have come close to generating on our own.

In fact, Cantor and his team might well have made the greatest mistake of their collective political lives, for with the "liberal professor" ad, we now had the opportunity to fully exploit the issue on which Cantor was most vulnerable: character. Unwittingly, he had taken hold of a live grenade. We just had to pull the pin and detonate it before June 10—Primary Day—and he would be exposed for the shameless liar he was: not just this lie, but his entire record.

GRAY'S TAKE

Every good campaign attracts characters; it means you're generating interest. If you don't draw your fair share of characters, it means you're probably running a lousy campaign.

Yet time is limited, and lots of people stop by the office with ideas and suggestions, and it is crucial to quickly differentiate between the doers and the talkers.

Talkers? We had a pair of volunteers nicknamed Batman and Robin by one of our county coordinators, whose photos could go alongside the term in the dictionary. This pair was sure they knew how to win this race, had a voter outreach strategy all mapped out, and supposedly had the background and expertise to back up their bravado. And, frankly, we were sucking wind in their county and needed help. So Zach and I gave them a lot of time—at first.

It all sounded too good to be true, and of course it was. Two weeks later, not a single door had not been knocked, nor a single phone call made.

Their excuse? They hadn't been trained on our database system. I wasted several more hours trying to walk them through that before throwing in the towel.

That was fine with them—they had a new idea, a plan to have huge BRAT signs put up throughout the district. That we had so few signs was driving Batman and Robin crazy, as it was some of our other volunteers. In our financial situation, signs were simply a low priority. But Batman and Robin promised that signs wouldn't cost the campaign a dime: They would raise the money themselves. Not incidentally, letting them do so would keep them busy and out of our hair.

So we said fine. Why not? Go ahead.

Huge mistake.

They did indeed raise funds for the signs, soliciting it from several other counties in return for the promise of an allotment of signs in those areas. But when the signs arrived, weeks late, they were folded in half and all but unusable. Worse, rather than hand them out according to who had donated the most money, or by the population of the county, Batman and Robin allotted them equally to all counties. The original contributors were furious. Charges flew from people who felt they'd been misled. It was a nightmare. All over the district, our people were at one another's throats. We had to devote precious hours to calming the waters.

Lesson learned. Never smile and nod and think a problem will go away—especially not when there's a rogue volunteer nodding back.

There was another volunteer, really nice guy. Turned out he was a hoarder—had stuff piled literally to the ceiling. But extremely committed. He'd regularly show up at the office with ancient printers and other equipment that didn't work.

One day, going over voter data, we spotted his name—one of our other volunteers had happened to knock on his door. In her notes, the volunteer wrote that she'd talked to him for quite a long time and that although "he didn't commit . . . I think I convinced him to vote for Brat."

That's right—the guy had been a volunteer with the campaign for months and never gave so much as a hint. Go figure.

TEN

"DAVE, YOU'RE GOING TO WIN THIS THING"

We began push polling—that is, polling with the intent of pushing our candidate and message—with about six weeks to go.

For the uninitiated, both parts of the term "push polling" are more or less accurate. Each of the four rounds of recorded calls we made to Seventh District voters leading up to the election was a sort of poll, though not one detailed or selective enough that it would be taken as statistically reliable by anyone with expertise in the field. (Hey, what do you want for $3,000 a pop?) But it suited our purpose, which was to have a sense of how the race was developing from week to week and to gauge the effectiveness of our messaging and other efforts with the voters.

In fact, it was the "push" part—how effective the "questions" were at nudging voters our way—that mattered more. Though many voters find such calls and their tiresome directives—"Press 1 if you agree; press 2 if you disagree; press 3 if you're undecided"—deeply annoying and hang up instantly, a surprising number stick it out to the end; in which case push polls can be highly effective in moving the needle.

Obviously, it's all about the phrasing of the "questions" and the order in which they're presented.

It's no accident that *questions* is set in quotation marks. Quite simply, their intent was to introduce damaging information about Cantor. Were they accurate? Sure—as far as they went. Were they impartial? Are you kidding? Take, for instance, a query on Cantor's having voted to fully fund Obamacare. How much good would it have done to ask "Did you know that to keep the government from closing, Eric Cantor had to compromise and vote to fund Obamacare?"

Compare that to how we actually asked the question: "Do you approve of Eric Cantor voting to fully fund Obamacare in November of last year?"

The bottom line—and what we wanted voters to know, without Cantor's political doublespeak excuses—is that he caved on Obamacare. All's fair in war, especially since the Cantor campaign was working fervently to make sure the voters did *not* know precisely that.

Our initial poll was conducted from May 1 to May 3:

BRAT—VA: VA07 Phone Poll		
Call Progress		
Live Person:	8,381	58%
Answering Machine:	2,504	18%
Fax:	77	1%
Busy:	44	0%
No Answer:	717	5%
Problem:	2,629	18%
Total:	14,352	

Q 1: Would you vote for Brat or Cantor?		
1: Brat	352	26%
2: Cantor	713	53%
3: Undecided	290	21%
Total:	1,355	

Q 2: Do you approve of Cantor submitting and voting for a bill that fully funded Obamacare last year?		
1: Approve	217	20%
2: Disapprove	700	65%
3: Undecided	163	15%
Total:	1,080	

Q 3: Do you approve of Cantor voting for the debt ceiling increase in January of this year?		
1: Approve	326	35%
2: Disapprove	450	48%
3: Undecided	161	17%
Total:	937	

Q 4: Do you approve of Cantor hiding a provision granting amnesty to illegal immigrants?		
1: Approve	155	18%
2: Disapprove	548	64%
3: Undecided	153	18%
Total:	856	

Q 5: After hearing these facts, would you vote for Brat or Cantor?		
1: Brat	351	42%
2: Cantor	301	36%
3: Undecided	183	22%
Total:	835	

Q 6: What is your gender?		
1: Male	366	46%
2: Female	431	54%
Total:	797	

On the face of it, these results are nothing short of stunning. If they are to be believed, within the space of a three-minute phone call, these voters went from favoring Cantor by a 56–23 margin with 21 percent undecided, to favoring Brat over Cantor by a margin of 42–36, with 22 percent undecided. Cantor loses 20 points, we gain 19, and there we are! It would be the political equivalent of a magic bullet, with the only ones truly firm in their convictions being the undecided!

Alas, what they mainly proved is that voters are fickle. How they answer a drive-by phone poll cannot be taken at face value. Though they obviously overwhelmingly disapproved of Cantor's positions on all of the Big Three issues—amnesty, Obamacare, and the debt—five to ten minutes later they could watch a Cantor commercial on TV and just as easily be swung back the other way. Probably, in at least some cases, sensing by the end that the poll had been generated by the Brat campaign, they said they supported Dave just to be nice. Virginians tend to be very nice people. Moreover, the numbers were certainly skewed, as Cantor zombies likely could not stand hearing the truth about their Dear Leader and would hang up, so not be reflected in the final result.

But while the numbers couldn't be trusted as statistical doctrine, they were not totally meaningless. What they showed beyond any question was that the race was fluid. Though a great many voters did not know much about Dave Brat or his positions, a clear majority were open to hearing more about Dave, and about Cantor's duplicities, and having their minds changed. Though they had known Eric Cantor for more than a decade, most were prepared to leave him high and dry if given good enough reason. Even when someone indicated they were a Cantor supporter, if they stuck with the call through all the damaging questions there proved an excellent chance that by the end they would be undecided or even say they were voting for Dave.

In short, the poll fully confirmed what we'd been picking up from our ground forces: The first half of the Herculean lift, turning a large bloc of Cantor's regular voters against him, was eminently doable.

From the looks of it, Cantor's floor was in the low forties—political junkie talk meaning the minimum percentage Cantor would get was between 40 and 44 percent. These were his diehards, the Cantor zombies. If they weren't swayed by his positions on Obamacare, immigration, or the debt, we'd never get them, not even if he were caught on video drop-kicking a puppy down Pennsylvania Avenue or serving as Obama's uniformed valet on Air Force One.

To repeat the refrain from Tom White's "Cantor Zombie":

I'll sell my soul and vote for him
And swear I won't get fooled again.

Humor, it's always effective—once they're laughing at you, you're dead.

Our second poll, conducted a week after the first, substituted a question on the STOCK Act for the one on the debt ceiling and tried different wording for the one on Obamacare. We wanted to see whether the new wording and questions would be more effective than what we were already asking, but the results changed little.

BRAT—VA: CD07 Poll		
Call Progress		
Live Person:	11,938	62%
Answering Machine:	2,384	12%
Fax:	154	1%
Busy:	89	0%
No Answer:	971	5%
Problem:	3,734	20%
Total:	19,270	

Q1: In the Republican Primary, for whom would you vote?		
1: Brat	461	27%
2: Cantor	874	51%
3: Undecided	373	22%
Total:	1,708	

Q2: Approve or disapprove of Cantor changing the STOCK Act?		
1: Approve	210	16%
2: Disapprove	743	58%
3: Undecided	326	26%
Total:	1,279	

Q3: Approve or disapprove of Cantor submitting and voting to fund Obamacare?		
1: Approve	355	31%
2: Disapprove	562	50%
3: Undecided	219	19%
Total:	1,136	

Q4: Approve or disapprove of Cantor hiding a provision to grant amnesty to illegal immigrants?		
1: Approve	218	22%
2: Disapprove	538	53%
3: Undecided	251	25%
Total:	1,007	

Q5: After hearing these facts, for whom would you vote?		
1: Brat	393	40%
2: Cantor	378	39%
3: Undecided	208	21%
Total:	979	

Q6: What is your gender?		
1: Male	416	45%
2: Female	515	55%
Total:	931	

But that did nothing to dampen our spirits. As more and more people tuned in, we were feeling a victory materializing on the ground. Voters just didn't like Cantor. After being introduced to Dave, they did like him, and they responded well to his message. We were getting this both from those going door to door and seeing it first-hand at events around the district.

Ron Hedlund was probably the first to risk saying it aloud. As he recalls it, one evening, after another long, successful day campaigning alongside the candidate, he turned to Dave: "Dave, listen, you're going to win this thing. I know it. Don't ask me how I know it, but I do. This is a done deal. You've won."

How could he be so sure?

> It was a spiritual thing. A day or two before, I was taking a shower and it just hit me like a ton of bricks. After all this stress, everything we'd been going through, I just knew, and I start crying like a baby. I mean, I was sobbing— sobbing so loud my wife came running into the bathroom to see what the heck was going on. Because there was no ambiguity here; it was good versus evil, and now I knew.

> After that, I just had a sense of calmness and serenity. It didn't mean we could sit back; we still had to work our butts off to get it done. But I wasn't worried about anything. At that point, even Dave didn't expect it, but I knew it was going to happen.

ELEVEN

THE ESTABLISHMENT LOSES ITS COOL

Republican district conventions, held every two years in each of Virginia's eleven congressional districts, are a huge deal. Their function is to choose the district chairmen, who in turn determine how the party is to be run within their districts—who is to be favored with party cash, patronage, and assorted other goodies. District chairs are like medieval dukes, dispensing favors and bribes and, when necessary, using force to maintain control over their fiefdoms. It hardly needs to be said that in the Seventh Congressional District, that individual, Linwood Cobb, was hand-picked by Cantor himself. Cobb was a veteran Cantor machine apparatchik (Sovietese for "hack") whose job basically consisted of seeing to it that the district's various county Republican committees stayed in line.

This year, the Seventh District Convention was scheduled for May 10, exactly one month before Primary Day. If the Henrico Mass

Meeting six weeks earlier had been the preliminary, this would be the main event. Emboldened by the earlier victory, the grassroots throughout the district were mobilized, and *we* were coming en masse.

The way these district conventions work is that the delegates elected by the County Mass Meetings gather, elect a temporary chair, and then elect the new district chair. Generally, the results of these meetings are preordained, with one side holding such numerical superiority that the results are as formulaic as basic arithmetic. And generally, our side isn't the one that has the numbers.

Not this time.

Frankly, we regarded the approaching convention with some ambivalence. Many of our key volunteers—individuals we relied on to bring in new recruits, make phone calls, and knock on doors— instead spent countless hours preparing for the convention, recruiting, calling, and visiting the homes of the potential delegates. Worse, much of this activity occurred out of our office! "What are they doing?" we thought. "Don't they know how much more important it is to defeat Eric Cantor than Linwood Cobb?" And winning the convention would be an uphill battle; pouring so many resources into the fight seemed wasteful, even foolhardy.

In retrospect, that was naive, shortsighted, and just plain wrong. Quite simply, we completely failed to appreciate the importance this convention would play in our election just a month later.

Unlike the Mass Meeting, the Cantor forces weren't going to be taken by surprise. Arriving at the Richmond Hilton, our people were met with a vast sea of Cantor signs—thousands of them, planted into every available square inch of lawn, not just on the road leading into the hotel, but on the businesses adjacent to the convention and along the main approach through town! The intended message—thanks again, Ray Allen—was one of inevitability. Here was yet more evidence, in case anyone on our side had forgotten for even a moment, of what the Cantor campaign had that ours never would: weight, substance, and overwhelming presence. They had their ads all over the radio and television, all their direct mail clogging voters' mailboxes, and—yes—all the yard signs anyone could dream of. They had *everything*, and all the money they needed to buy more. We could knock on all the doors we wanted, but in the end, it was peashooters against tanks, and Cantor would win like he always did.

The truth? Turning a corner and being confronted with the massive display did give pause, at least momentarily. It was pretty awe-inspiring, probably the most impressive such display ever seen in the district. From the look of it, there was hardly a square inch left for Brat signs—even if we could have afforded them.

But the intimidation factor wasn't what Ray Allen hoped it would be. If Cantor's people expected the display to give rise to defeatism, they didn't know our grassroots. The morning before the convention, a smattering of defiant Brat signs appeared in the midst of Cantor's armada. It turned out volunteers from Chesterfield County had dug into their own pockets and had them rush-printed.

Cantor's campaign was loaded for bear. It bused in hundreds of bought-and-paid-for "supporters," providing them with free food and lodging. Linwood Cobb had a promotional piece, a five-page multifold, high-color, high-gloss job that might have cost more than we'd spent to date on our entire campaign. Aimed at blowing any potential rival out of the water, the magazine-quality brochure included endorsements from every elected official of any note in the district.

And that was just the part where they were more or less playing by the rules. As we well knew, at previous conventions Ray Allen had had his flunkies play all sorts of dirty games; once they even cut the power to the PA system when opponents spoke. And already this time, they'd switched the event's venue, taking their sweet time before letting those of us on the other side know, hoping the move from a local high school to the Hilton would sow confusion and hamper our efforts. Then they had booked almost all the hotel's available rooms for their own people—a price tag our campaign could only pay in Zimbabwian currency.

Though the convention was only a one-day event, this created logistical problems for our side—and, when it didn't, the Cantor campaign took further measures to make sure it did. Most notably, they attempted to sabotage the "Empty Chair Debate," a stunt we'd planned wherein Dave would debate an empty chair, dramatizing Cantor's refusal to take Dave on *mano a mano*. Learning of the switch in venue, one of our activists had immediately called the hotel and reserved a large room for the event. But by the time we arrived to pay the reservation fee, we were told the room was no longer available. Instead, we ended up holding the debate in the parking lot of Honey Baked Ham, a restaurant across the street from the hotel.

Rumor had it Ray Allen and other high-level Cantor staffers could see our little "debate"—which wound up with close to 200 attendees—out the window of the hotel while drinking their morning coffee.

The Cantor machine's usual method was to get its way by sheer force of authority. They were the power elite; deference to their will by lesser mortals had always been their presumed right. Delegates to these conventions did what they were told because of who was doing the telling.

Yet this time, as they watched even more people navigate the minefield of yard signs heading to the hotel, it was clear the Cantor people were starting to get concerned. There were a lot more of us than they'd expected, and, more to the point, this year's breed of grassroots types seemed a lot less easily intimidated than usual. Nearly every other delegate was defiantly sporting a Brat sticker.

Once the convention was formally under way, Allen's operatives were everywhere in evidence, buttonholing delegates, trying to nail down votes for Linwood Cobb. But Allen and company were infuriated that they'd even have to go through the democratic motions. Early on, one of our supporters reported spotting Ray Allen in the hall, gesticulating and swearing wildly as he talked to Kristi Way, Cantor's chief of staff, indifferent to a bunch of little kids passing by with their parents.

The machine had lost its infamous cool.

Soon, like dogs returning to their vomit, they resorted to their familiar tactics. Making up rules along the way, they challenged the credentials of some of our key people, insisting they weren't authorized to participate. Had it been anyone else pulling this, it would have defied belief; with these guys, it was just business as usual. And why not? Hadn't it always worked in the past?

But not this time. This convention was not about to be stampeded. The Cantor rent-a-supporters may have had noisemakers and whistles—they came in their goodie bags, along with food and bottled water—but with lungpower to spare, our people matched them decibel for decibel.

Incredibly, among those the Cantor people insisted had no right to appear was—Dave Brat. It took us presenting them with a copy of the rules before Dave was allowed to speak.

Dave set the crowd roaring, going as hard as he ever had against crony capitalism; Washington, D.C.; and the constant lies of the Cantor campaign. This time Eric Cantor was in the room to hear him, in the front row, along with his wife and children, and he had to listen as Dave declared his actions on the STOCK Act "an impeachable offense."

Following with his own speech, Cantor tried to hit back hard, repeating the "liberal professor" line his campaign had used so often before. But he'd never before faced an audience like this one, and the charge was greeted now with all the respect it deserved—drawing loud boos and raucous shouts of "Liar!" and "Debate!" Cantor was stunned. As soon as he finished, visibly angry, he beat a graceless retreat.

It all led up to the vote for district chairman. Our candidate, Fred Gruber, was a patriot but, let's just say, a bit rough around the edges. A stubborn, plainspoken old ex-Marine, while speaking at a recent gathering in New Kent County, he'd offhandedly described the fancy black SUVs favored by Cantor and Cobb as "government Nazi cars." To belabor the obvious: It's *never* smart to compare anyone or anything to Nazis, and it didn't help that Eric Cantor was Jewish. That such a figure as Fred Gruber would even dare challenge Linwood Cobb as the district's Republican leader was seen by the other side as an abomination.

But in his appearance before the crowd assembled for the convention, fitted out in a suit purchased a day earlier, delivering the speech he had reluctantly promised to rehearse ten times, Fred did just fine.

His performance may not have been polished, like Cobb's, but that wasn't a bad thing. Cobb looked like what he is, too smooth, oozing faux sincerity from every pore; but Fred, take him or leave him, was the genuine article.

Fred Gruber: The Establishment's worst nightmare

The vote was by paper ballot, and Ron Hedlund was among our representatives charged with distributing them to eligible delegates. When he finished distributing them, he still had some blank ballots in hand.

"I'll take those," he heard someone say.

Ron almost had to laugh at the brazenness. It was none other than Henrico County Sheriff Mike Wade, a well known high-level cog in the Cantor machine. And he wasn't even among those appointed to oversee the vote tally.

"Sorry," Ron said, "but I don't think so." That evening, although by then things were settled, Ron took the excess ballots home with him—just to be sure.

The final tally, in the weighted voting: Fred Gruber, 675.8; Linwood Cobb, 630.

Incredible!

As we celebrated that evening with hugs, laughs, and beer, some of the young Cantor "volunteers" were literally in tears. Not that you could blame them—they still had all those signs to pick up.

True to form, the *Times-Dispatch* ignored this startling development in their own backyard. But the story did receive major play on a few conservative web sites. "Tea Party Boos, Heckles Eric Cantor in His Home District—and That Wasn't Even the Worst of It" a headline in the *Blaze* put it.

Even more telling was a story on *PJ Media* a few days later. Headlined "After Eric Cantor Loss, Ray Allen Pledges to Bankrupt the Republican Party of Virginia," it reported:

> House Majority Leader Eric Cantor's long-time top con-
> sultant, Ray Allen, has "angrily" stated to multiple indi-
> viduals that he intends to bankrupt the Republican Party
> of Virginia (RPV), to install his own people throughout all
> levels of RPV's State Central Committee, and to rebuild
> the RPV with money from Eric Cantor's donors. Ray Allen
> is considered the "brain trust" of Eric Cantor's Young
> Guns, which has spent hundreds of thousands of dollars
> and has hired staff with the intention of retaking control
> of the RPV at all levels . . . . In this effort to reclaim the
> majority, Ray Allen has helped orchestrate the parliamen-

tary procedure of "slating" at several RPV conventions this season . . . [H]undreds to thousands of Tea Party/conservative delegates have been forcefully ejected from VA RPV conventions over the past few weeks and months. However, the ejected delegates and others opposed to Team Cantor have since had success appealing the slating attempts, leaving Allen and Cantor with little to show for their hardball tactics other than alienated constituents, a terrible local public relations problem, and worse, a rapidly gaining primary opponent in challenger Dave Brat.

For those perceptive enough to see—which excluded the entire mainstream press—something momentous was bubbling up the Seventh District.

Asked to comment on sore loser Ray Allen's bitter vow to undo the results of the convention, Dave issued the following statement:

> I cannot emphasize this enough: the Republican Party of Virginia will never again be a strong, unified party until it rids itself of Eric Cantor and Ray Allen.
>
> With those two around, forget any talk of mending the rift in the GOP, or of creating a "big tent"—these guys want a two-person tent. And we learn today that you, the constituents, are being treated as an obstacle towards reaching that goal, and not as their employers.
>
> I am here to unify the party, to strengthen the party, to be a powerful representative voice for the Seventh District

GOP, and to serve all Seventh District citizens no matter their party affiliation. A public servant, as per the intent of the House's existence.

Perfect.

ZACH'S TAKE

The Seventh District Convention was the first and only time I met, or even saw, Eric Cantor during the entire campaign. I was with Dave and Laura Brat when all at once Laura decides she's going to confront Cantor on his absurd television ads. So we weave our way through the Capital Police escort and throngs of loyal Cantorites, and when we finally get over to him, she says, "Eric, you have got to stop running those ads with my husband as a cartoon. It's getting my kids made fun of at school, and it's just mean and nasty and completely untrue, and you know it." Eric Cantor just looked at her blankly for a good five or ten seconds and didn't say a word. So finally Dave and Laura just walked away in disgust.

This left just myself and Cantor, standing about three feet apart. I was wearing a badge saying "Brat Campaign Staff," so he looked at that, and then slowly looked up, stopping at my face, and he asked, with this sinister sneer, "What's your name?"

I stuck my hand out. "Zach Werrell–pleasure to meet you, Mr. Cantor." For a moment he just stared back at me with these big black, dead great white shark eyes, then he offered this limp hand. It was really unsettling–I had the feeling that he'd devour me, if given half the chance.

GRAY'S TAKE

During the convention, I went up to say hello to one of Cantor's people, Joe Ellison, with whom I'd worked on the E. W. Jackson campaign. We got to talking, and I'd never been so condescended to in my life. It was like, "Oh, well, Gray, it's really nice you have a job and all, and keep up the fight. But you guys don't really think you stand a chance in hell, do you? Cantor's polling is showing he's up 80-20."

I said, "Joe, I don't think that's even close to true, but you can keep believing what you want to believe."

At which point the veneer of civility completely dropped: "I don't know what you're doing working against Cantor, but you're never going to have a job in politics again."

"Right," I said, "just like we don't have any chance of winning this convention."

But that was the mentality of Cantor's people. A month before the primary, and they never saw it coming. To them, it wasn't even remotely within the realm of possibility that Eric Cantor might lose—not within a hundred thousand miles.

And the only thing I was thinking at that moment was: *Great, keep it up—that's only going to help us.*

TWELVE

MOMENTUM SHIFT

The Cantor campaign was quick to dismiss their defeat at the convention as no big deal—just a bunch of right-wing nuts and "hicks from Hanover" who mobilized for a one-day event and got lucky. "Our polling is showing that a vast majority of Tea Party supporters and members support Eric Cantor," assured Ray Allen, "and we're looking forward to a resounding victory on June 10th."

In fact, their internal polling did show them far up, if not nearly by the 80–20 margin they claimed.

But in insisting they weren't at least a little shaken by what happened, either they were dumber than we thought or even bigger liars. Arrogant as they were, they had to be sensing some of what we were feeling more strongly every day: that the tide was starting to turn in our direction.

Indeed, now almost every time Ron Hedlund came to the office, he'd give a cockeyed smile and wryly declare: "You've got this in the bag."

While this nearly drove us to ban him from the office permanently on the grounds he would jinx us, it was also great to hear. Hey, with a budget as tight as ours, how could we afford to turn down positive vibes?

Still, the world continued to take the Cantor forces at their word, which was a real problem for us. Their absolute and total confidence that they would crush us kept us from receiving much-needed support from a number of key groups. First on that list was the National Rifle Association. For the NRA, the race should have been an easy call. Dave is an uncompromising Second Amendment advocate down the line, and Cantor was Cantor—which is to say, likely to go wobbly when it counted most. Once already he'd betrayed the NRA, as a member of the Virginia House of Delegates voting for the reviled "One Gun a Month" legislation.

They endorsed Cantor.

Dave's positions on the issues were never the main consideration; Dave was 100 percent pro-gun, and the NRA still stonewalled us. What counted was Cantor's power and his readiness to use it to threaten and intimidate.

If no one's ever before accused the NRA of being wimps, count this as an historic first. As an excuse for supporting the less gun-friendly candidate, they lamely offered that they hadn't received Dave's candidate survey in time—leading to the suspicion that Allen and Cantor might have induced them to "lose" it. Ron Hedlund (who's not just a lifetime member of the NRA, but an *endowed* lifetime member) got on the case, providing a regional representative he knew with documentation establishing that the NRA survey had been mailed up to national headquarters in plenty of time. We had the FedEx receipt showing it had been signed for, for crying out loud. Still, no dice. After first not returning his calls, the NRA finally removed from their website the claim that Dave Brat had stiffed them by not returning the survey, and allowed us to resubmit the survey. But by then the damning misinformation had already been up for several days, which was very, very bad. Gun people are committed—and they vote.

We also thought we had an excellent shot at the endorsement of the National Federation of Independent Businesses, especially after being told by their local representative that the endorsement was a done deal. But he got overruled by the state and national organization. The reason given? Although Eric Cantor was not entirely to their liking, he was not just any incumbent; he was *Eric Cantor*.

Then—talk about a natural fit—there was Tea Party Patriots, the umbrella organization for over 2,000 local groups nationally. They considered helping us, and when we met with Jenny Beth Martin, their president, we laid it all out. We readily admitted that if they did a phone poll, it would probably show Cantor well ahead—but they shouldn't believe the poll, because it didn't reflect what we were seeing in the field. We explained that pollsters cannot call cell phones, so older people, Cantor's strongest constituency, and far more likely than other demographics to have landlines, were being overcounted.

We even pointed out that there were some voters on our side who, assuming we lacked the money for such an exercise, would think the polling was coming from Cantor's camp, so would be deliberately sabotaging the results. We told the Tea Party Patriots we were bringing new primary voters to the process, fed-up conservatives who don't normally vote in these primaries because they don't think there's anyone to vote for. What mattered was that the electorate was moving our way; as the campaign was progressing, we were seeing more and more people, especially younger people, enthusiastically calling out their support in the street, and drivers giving us the thumbs-up. And we were getting an overwhelmingly positive response on social media. Only recently, we'd put the word out on Facebook that people should chalk paint their car windows with "Vote Dave Brat, June 10," and now the done-up windows were everywhere.

No matter—Tea Party Patriots did a poll that showed us way down, and they drew back.

Same story with the Club for Growth—their polling also showed us too far down to merit consideration as one of their targeted races.

We *knew* the polling data was skewed. It *had* to be, because it failed to reflect what we were seeing on the ground. That went even for our own polling; after the triumph at the district meeting, it showed us with only a slight boost.

Frankly, seeing bad numbers over and over could get unsettling. But we had to brush them off: Even admitting the possibility that these numbers were accurate meant we might lose, and that was unthinkable. Better they prod us to work even harder over the last three weeks.

Of course, it wasn't only organizations that could be made to keep us at arm's length. The Brats had close friends, members of the Country Club of Virginia and the Dominion Country Club set, who lived near them in a beautiful multi-million-dollar home. Sometimes Dave headed over there after work to meet Laura and the kids and to relax over a drink and cigars. The family scheduled a fundraiser for early May that we were hoping might be a rare big-money event for us. Then, just a couple of weeks before, the wife called Laura Brat and backed out. She told Laura that when she started making calls, she kept hearing the same thing: "You're going against Eric Cantor? Are you nuts?" She got so scared they shut it down. They ended up writing Dave a $2,000 check instead.

Disheartening as such a betrayal was—and, given our financial circumstances, as painful—it was more than matched by how much others sacrificed for this campaign. One evening, for example, totaling up the checks after a backyard barbecue, we were stunned to find a check for a thousand dollars from a woman we knew to be of modest means, whose daughter had been in Dave's class. Proportionally, that donation was probably the equivalent of a million from the well-to-do couple.

If something like that doesn't drive you to keep going, nothing will.

In the wake of Dave's victory, it would be mentioned frequently that of the $380,000 we had raised—against Cantor's $5.2 million, plus untold millions more spent on his behalf by others—almost all of it came in small donations.

As for the Cantor campaign's spending versus ours, the cliches apply at both ends: They spent like drunken sailors; we tossed around nickels like manhole covers. In fact, we were so intent on shepherding our scarce resources that we didn't run our first radio ad until thirty days out from the primary. Even then, it was a miniscule ad buy— just $2,000. The idea was to at least put up *something*, as encouragement for our volunteers. We had to show we had at least *some* money, that we could hit back a *little*.

The focus of that first ad was a no-brainer: Average voters, the sort who don't pay close attention, were being deluged by television ads and slick literature promoting Cantor as "leading the fight against President Barack Obama's liberal agenda," "leading the fight against Obamacare," and "leading the fight against Obama's imperial presidency"—and they needed to hear the other side. That first ad, citing Cantor's voting record on immigration, Obamacare, and spending, basically said that where Cantor was, in fact, leading America was into the toilet.

We quickly followed with a second ad. This one reflected our belief that in a media-saturated age, fancy production values can actually be a liability. It was simply Dave speaking for a full minute. He addressed the liberal professor smear, then returned to the Big Three issues and what he would do differently. The contrast with Cantor, who in his ads always hid behind an announcer's voiceover, was stark.

This ad was so effective that we kept running it until the end of the campaign. Having at first advertised just on WRVA 1140, the main conservative talk station in Richmond, we now also bought time on Kiss Liberty FM, a women-oriented light rock station, as well as several large country stations in Spotsylvania and Fredericksburg and ESPN radio.

Incredibly—or maybe not, given the disparity in resources—the "liberal professor" lie was still hurting us. In some of their recent print pieces, they had actually elevated Dave's status to "radical professor Dave Brat."

Of course, our volunteers had been working hard to set the record straight, and we were also fighting back on social media. In fact, in a neat bit of table-turning, some of our people had been getting Cantor supporters to admit how preposterous the charge was. Kim was particularly adept at this. "'Hey, Buddy,'" as she describes her initial approach to pro-Cantor Virginia state delegate Buddy Fowler via email, "'I'm a constituent of yours, and I have a question. I really trust you, Buddy, and I'm trying to sift through all these mailings and these ads about Dave Brat. You've known Dave for a while—he's not really liberal, is he? Because I just can't make any sense of it. So what's your opinion on Dave, Buddy?' And, in a stand-up move, he comes out and says, of course, Dave Brat is not a liberal."

Deb Wetlaufer, a Hanover volunteer, went to work on Hanover House of Delegates member Chris Peace. She approached him respectfully and simply asked, "Do you believe that Dave Brat is a liberal like Cantor is asserting in his television ads?"

Peace replied, "Deb, thanks for asking. I spoke to Gerry Baugh the other day and suggested to him that when one is asked to serve, many feel compelled to that service by a sense of duty and honor as a Virginian. Heck, it may be possible that with a seat at the table, a conservative could rein in some of the excess. Overall, I think the allegations are a stretch. I have known David Brat for a long time and have never thought he is a liberal professor. In fact, his ethics as a seminarian and economist have always been very impressive to me."

And then former Cantor advisor Amanda Chase also admitted, "it's a complete lie."

So we took all their quotes on the subject and used them on our only glossy mail piece.

The truth is, for a campaign of such a supposedly smart candidate, the Cantor machine continually helped us out by doing incredibly stupid things. Cantor refused to debate us. Fine, no problem, that's what frontrunners often do—except in this case, by demonstrating Dave Brat's availability to voters and his openness to their concerns, it emphasized Cantor's inaccessibility and lack of empathy. We were holding town halls throughout the district, something the voters had long forgotten about. Dave took any question and answered it, in stark contrast to the way Cantor conducted his: scripted questions, scripted answers. Silence from the peanut gallery.

Cantor should have cut his losses right there and simply ignored Dave's appearances around the district. Instead, his campaign often sent surrogates to appear on his behalf. And not just any surrogates, but—invariably—inept and unprepared surrogates. (But okay, let's give them the benefit of the doubt: They were probably the only ones willing to be recruited for the thankless task.)

Take, for instance, the elected Hanover County supervisor who spoke for Cantor one evening at an event in Culpepper. She had literally nothing to say beyond bumper sticker pablum: "Eric Cantor is fighting for us, and he's a true conservative. He believes that every American should be able to find a good-paying job." After that uninspiring drivel, Dave stood up and began ripping into Cantor on issue after issue. She had no facts with which to answer back. We were watching, and actually began to feel sorry for this woman. The low ebb was the Q&A, when someone stood up and asked her about NSA spying—which was in the news just then—and she proclaimed, "Eric Cantor does not condone spying on Americans and never would!" So Dave picked up our comparison sheet and read to the crowd how Cantor had just voted *against* the Justin Amash amendment to restrict phone monitoring to only those suspected of terrorism. The ignorance and dishonesty of Cantor's representative was so naked people just broke out laughing.

After all, everyone in that room knew full well why she was subjecting herself to such humiliation: It was a career move, a shot at moving up the chain. She figured if she was willing to take the hits for Eric, he'd remember a few months later when she ran for delegate, or a few years after that if she hoped to run for Congress. She wanted Cantor's seal of approval and, equally, Cantor's money.

The Cantor campaign also dispatched others to our events to record every word Dave spoke in the hope they'd catch him saying something that could be twisted or misrepresented and turned into a flub to be exploited in fliers and ads. Aside from refusing to debate his opponent on the issues—and refusing to honestly acknowledge major parts of his own record—the smear was Cantor's most reliable weapon. But Dave is a consummate pro, and never shot from the hip. It never happened.

The surest sign that momentum was shifting our way was the ever-increasing size of the crowds when Dave appeared at events—and the way they no longer hung back, waiting to be convinced, but instead made it clear they were already with us.

Take, for instance, the Beaverdam Wine Festival, a major annual event in the district featuring music, food, lots of wine, and, of course, thousands of voters. We brought a contingent to support and promote Dave. But, more important, we brought Dave himself.

Naturally, Eric Cantor was hundreds—possibly thousands—of miles away. A couple of Cantor's usual paid "volunteers" were there in his stead. Stationed in one of the first booths you saw when you walked into the place, they dutifully handed out Cantor stickers without any pretense of enthusiasm: just kids doing a job, putting in the least possible effort. Even so, it was striking how almost no one wanted their stickers: Literally, they couldn't give them away. After a couple of hours, the two of them threw in the towel. They wandered over to the wine tent and used their tickets to get glasses of wine. It was as though they were saying: "Hey, we did two hours' work. Good enough—let's party!"

Our volunteers, meanwhile, were walking around stickering the whole place. Before long, it seemed like most everyone at the festival had on a Dave Brat sticker. It began looking like the Dave Brat Wine Festival. Dave was talking to people left and right, getting his back slapped and slapping others', and loving every minute of it. We all were.

Photo by Ron Hedlund

So we decided we would try to finish the job, go for a clean sweep. In terms of signage, the festival was the opposite of the district convention: There was only one Cantor sign in evidence. A girl in the wine tent had it. So one of our volunteers went over and asked, "Can I buy your Cantor sign?"

"How much?"

"Five bucks?"

"Sure!" she said, handing it over before he could change his mind.

At that point, there looked to be just one remaining holdout: an older gentleman sporting his Cantor sticker.

Dave took on this one personally.

"I see you've got a Cantor sticker there," he said, approaching the man.

Yes, he had, the guy agreed; he was a longtime supporter of the congressman. "Eric Cantor has a lot of influence, and that's something we shouldn't lose. As a veteran, I rely on him to protect our benefits."

These were common arguments on Cantor's behalf, of course.

"Well—did you know that Cantor voted against veteran's benefits?" asked Dave, perfectly replicating a push poll question.

"Really?"

Dave proceeded to lay out the particulars, the specific bill involved, and the back room maneuvering behind it. Then he went into the Republican Creed and how Cantor had failed nearly every test on the list; and he talked about the importance of faith, morality and ethics in politics.

It took a good five minutes, but the gentleman heard Dave out, listening very thoughtfully. When Dave finished, there was a long pause. Then, slowly, the old man peeled off his Cantor sticker, and Dave handed him a Brat sticker that he put in its place.

GRAY'S TAKE

For all their initial doubts about my taking the job, once I was on board with the Brat campaign, my parents were all in–100 percent. And my mom proved to be one of our most effective volunteers.

She worked with a dear friend from Charlottesville, Chardon Jenks. They'd bonded for the cause during the E. W. Jackson campaign. Chardon is a truly remarkable person, a woman of deep faith and a real inspiration. Not long ago, she suffered several tragedies, losing both her husband and son, and she decided to dedicate her life to doing her part to save the country.

My mom and Chardon made a wonderful tag team. We assigned them a wealthy, Establishment precinct near the University of Richmond– the kind of neighborhood not many of our volunteers were comfortable working–and during crunch time, they were there almost every day, door knocking. If they didn't have a walk list on a particular day, they impro- vised, driving around picking out homes with American flags. Chardon would be behind the wheel, my mom would hop out. She has no fear. She'll naturally talk to anyone–she just likes people, and people see that. So a half hour later, Chardon often found herself still in the car, patiently waiting–planning their next neighborhood stop while my mom was hanging out in a living room.

Chardon is pretty effusive herself, so they never had to do a hard sell. They were just themselves, maybe talking generally about the state of the country. But, of course, eventually they'd get to the race and the contrast between the candidates.

When you got that tag team going, the other person didn't stand a chance—they'd be ready to vote for Dave Brat if only to not disappoint Chardon and my mother.

That was an important precinct, and a tough one for our campaign. It was the heart of Cantor country; his people expected to win it going away.

They didn't—it ended up close to dead even.

THIRTEEN

TURNING THE TABLES ON ALINSKY

Many people deserve credit for helping bring down Eric Cantor, and in the wake of Dave Brat's stunning victory, even more tried to claim it. But among the handful whose contributions are impossible to overstate are nationally syndicated talk radio hosts Laura Ingraham and Mark Levin. At long last, and in the proverbial nick of time, they succeeded in turning our local race national.

To be sure, both had long known Cantor for the phony he is, nailing him to the wall publicly for his galling duplicities even as too many other prominent conservatives gave the majority leader a "still-one-of-us" pass. A year and a half before our primary, Levin termed Cantor "a little weasel," railing at length against Cantor's latest RINO move, "a piece of ultra-left-wing trash dressed up as a violence against women law, which is a disaster, and [Cantor is] threatening conservatives who want to kill it." A noted constitutional scholar and head of the Landmark Legal Foundation, Levin added:

> We are not fooled by the title on this law. We are not fooled that aspects of it are unconstitutional and were ruled unconstitutional in the year 2000. And we are not fooled by the breadth of this law, which includes people who are not women, which confers jurisdiction in some cases to Indian tribes, which expands immigration for more illegal immigrants, and which has such ambiguous and vague language as "emotional distress" or "using unpleasant speech."

Noting that Cantor had cowed fellow Republicans into supporting the measure by threatening that killing legislation entitled the Violence Against Women Act would lead to a Republican "civil war," Levin bluntly called his bluff: "Mr. Cantor, I hate to tell you this: We're *already* in political war with you."

In early 2014, Cantor was again in Levin's crosshairs. When the Republican-led House buckled to pressure in February and voted to raise the debt ceiling without conditions, Levin nailed notorious crony capitalist Cantor as a lead culprit, scornfully telling his audience that the majority leader and his colleagues had proven "once again that they are not willing to fight, they do not consider your best interests in mind while claiming to represent you, and that they need to be voted out. The disparity between us and the ruling class is growing every day. They want to reconstruct our social system and bring the end of free market capitalism, as the debt will continue to rise if they allow it to." Then, in the weeks that followed, with nonstop reports of children streaming across our Southern border dominating the news, he zeroed in on Cantor's support of a version of "immigration reform" that looked suspiciously like the one being pushed by "open borders" liberals.

One afternoon in late April, once again going after Cantor, Levin blurted out in frustration: "Is anyone out there running against Cantor? Is *anyone?*"

Truly—and if ever there was a measure of how startlingly little notice the race had to date attracted outside the cocoon of Virginia's Seventh Congressional District—he seemed to have no idea.

Among his more than 200 broadcast outlets are Richmond's WRVA and WCHV in Charlottesville, and we started furiously dialing his call-in number—we can still repeat it by heart—on every available phone in the office. Within minutes, we were talking to his producer: "Yes, there is someone running! His name is Dave Brat, and we'd love to be on your show!"

They scheduled us immediately, for May 2, a Friday, at 8:30. It wasn't the greatest spot, but no matter. Mark Levin is extremely popular in Virginia, and that Friday, Dave was at his best. On the basis of that one brief appearance, we raised $26,000 from around the country, a huge number for us.

A couple of weeks later, Levin had us on again—which brought in another $40,000. And, for good measure, he put Dave on once more, right before the election.

At the same time, Laura Ingraham—who'd had Dave on her show very early in the campaign—was absolutely killing Cantor on immigration, making the case that Dave was the guy to beat him. In fact, Ingraham and Co. became so passionate about the campaign that her executive assistant began bombarding us with ideas for press releases and suggestions for sound bites that Dave might use in press conferences. All good ideas—if we'd only had a staff of, say, twenty-five . . .

But did their support ever pay off! It, too, began generating serious cash, and at the perfect time. Suddenly, with a couple of weeks to go, we found ourselves able to throw money at media. The cash was rolling in so fast that, from day to day, it was hard to keep track of how much we had in the bank. Some days it was, "Oh, crap—we have $6,000 more than we thought. Quick! Get a check over to the station!" In the last ten days, we ended up spending $60,000 on Clear Channel, buying time on WRVA and ESPN as well as on a couple of their music stations.

One radio ad in particular would end up being a difference maker, by far the most successful ad we ran in the entire campaign. As these stories so often go, it was the one that almost didn't happen. When we first broached the idea of a no-holds-barred ad attacking Cantor on crony capitalism, Dave was against it—not the premise, but the execution, as we had written it. He thought it might be seen as personally attacking Cantor on his net worth, like Obama smearing the one percent, especially with some voice-of-God narrator doing the attacking. It was a principled disagreement on both ends, but with time running short, and pressure building, it flared into a conflagration.

In the end, we came to a compromise. We ditched the voiceover and instead had a regular person, a real small business owner, do the talking. That was Dave's idea, and it was a really smart one. And Ken Davis was a perfect fit. He was our Chesterfield coordinator, and he used to own a business refurbishing and selling computers and printers —until he lost it in the economic downturn.

Ken couldn't have been better. His rich Southern accent, straight-forward words, and somewhat halting manner conveyed that this was not just another political pitch: It was a real person speaking from the heart, from hard personal experience, about how hard he'd worked building his business and how it all went down the drain.

Here's the exact script:

> My name is Ken Davis, a resident of Chesterfield County, and I had to close my small business due to our poor economy. While many small businesses were closing or downsizing, Congressman Cantor's net worth increased from approximately $2 million in 2008 to as much as $14 million today. At the same time, the average income of a middle class family declined by more than $4,300. Yet Eric Cantor is pushing for citizenship for illegal immigrants who take our jobs and reduce our take-home pay. I also googled the STOCK Act and saw that Eric Cantor changed the language of the bill to allow family members to continue insider trading on Congressional knowledge. If we inside trade, we go to jail! Members of Congress, their staff, and big business are exempt from the regulations of Obamacare, while small businesses are laying off employees due to the new law. Who is Eric Cantor representing? Not us. On June 10, it is time to tell Congressmen Cantor to play by the same rules as the voters of Virginia. Vote Dave Brat at your regular polling location on June 10.

We began airing the ad eight days before the election, and the response was unbelievable. Within minutes of the ad's first airing, we had listeners calling our campaign office telling us that we had just won the election.

We pushed that ad as hard as we could, in as many places as possible. The beauty of it was that we were using classic Alinsky tactics, straight out of *Rules for Radicals*, and were not the least bit ashamed of it!

In response, the Cantor machine freaked out. Within two hours of our ad's first appearance, they rushed a rebuttal ad onto the air with a deeply affronted announcer claiming our ad false and deceptive, accusing us of peddling internet conspiracy theories and false rumors. They then followed up with a literature piece entitled "Dave Brat's Lies." It claimed that insider trading has *always* been illegal and asked, "How could anyone calling himself an economist not know this?" Indeed, they said, our ad showed that Dave Brat got his information from internet rumors and chat room conspiracy theorists. And if you can't trust Dave Brat to even know what insider trading is, "How can you trust him on anything?"

It seemed like a particularly desperate act of misdirection. For, of course, what we were talking about wasn't civilian inside trading, Martha Stewart–style, but the congressional kind—and the extraordinary lengths to which Congressman Cantor went to make sure the gravy train kept rolling.

Cantor's was of course the classic tactic of seeking to muddy the waters with the message that *everyone* lies, *no one's* entirely trustworthy—so stick with our guy. The devil you know is better than the devil you don't. It is evidence, above all—the Clintons, anyone?—of Cantor's willingness to corrupt the public's own morality in the service of personal ambition.

No, there *was* a difference: Cantor was a liar, Brat wasn't, and that was the message we were determined to drive home. In those last couple of weeks, we spent another $15,000 on digital buys, most on a spot showing Cantor doing nothing *but* lying. There Cantor was in film clip after film clip, up close and personal, making claims—about Obamacare, immigration, the budget—that were readily contradicted by his votes. The spot ended with an especially earnest Cantor intoning, on CNBC no less, with great conviction, "Actions speak louder than words." "Yes, Congressman Cantor," agreed our narrator, "actions DO speak louder than words." A pause. "Vote Dave Brat."

Conversant Media told us they had never had a more successful buy than the ad exposing Cantor's lies, saying it played almost as well with Independents and Democrats as it did with Republicans. According to Conversant's data, more than 70 percent of those who clicked on the web version watched it all the way to the end, an incredible number. They told us that when they saw that figure, they knew we were going to win it.

It should be noted that our ads were uniformly produced on the cheap—which doesn't mean they looked or sounded cheap. Underfunded campaigns routinely spend $20,000 or $30,000 to have production or digital media companies do their TV ads--money flushed down the toilet. These days, everyone knows a capable video editor—ours was a Delany family friend, Allie Merrill—and the two of us wrote the ads, along with a couple of volunteers. Allie produced both television ads at a total cost of $3,000, and there was no discernible quality difference between our ads and Mitt Romney's.

With money to burn, the Cantor campaign's attacks on Dave only intensified in the last few weeks, with a slick new brochure turning up in district mailboxes seemingly daily. Now the charges they leveled were not just ludicrous, but contradictory. Cantor was still doggedly sticking with "liberal professor" Dave; one widely distributed brochure featured matching sinister-looking black-and-white shots of Dave, Barack Obama, and Democratic ex-governor Tim Kaine. At the same time, another brochure portrayed him as an out-of-control Tea Party crazy "Pushing a Plan to Cut Social Security."

And of course they sent one that just went out to seniors. On the front was a photograph of a mournful looking old couple, fronted by the medications "Radical Professor" Dave Brat allegedly wanted to take away from them.

RADICAL PROFESSOR DAVID BRAT

HE'S PUSHING A PLAN TO CUT SOCIAL SECURITY

David Brat is proposing a freeze on Social Security and Medicare spending. He even opposes the Medicare Part D Prescription Drug Benefit.

With over 300,000 people retiring every month, Brat's plan would mean immediate cuts to all Social Security checks for today's seniors.

Not only would David Brat's radical plan eliminate cost of living adjustments, his plan would mean an actual reduction in benefits of over $50 per month or $700 per year for today's seniors.

David Brat's plan to cut spending on Social Security and Medicare would be a disaster for seniors living on a fixed income.

Culpeper Star-Exponent
January 25, 2014
"Brat said as the campaign progressed he would put his pledges and promises on his web page including one that he not support any more entitlement spending for Medicare and Social Security..."

WECHECKTHEFACTS.COM

It asserted:

- David Brat is proposing a freeze on Social Security and Medicare spending. He even opposes Medicare Part D Prescription Drug Benefit.

- With over 300,000 people retiring every month, Brat's plan would mean immediate cuts to all Social Security checks for all today's seniors.

None of this was true. All of it was invented. Dave Brat hadn't even *offered* a plan involving Social Security or Medicare.

But it was on immigration that the slickster smear artist Ray Allen really outdid himself. With the endless news reports of small children heading north, we were brutalizing Cantor on the issue, and his longtime support of the Dream Act was clearly a serious liability. So, with little more than a week to go, who suddenly showed up in the district, injecting himself in the campaign? None other than Congressman Luis V. Gutierrez (D–IL), one of the most militant pro-amnesty pols in the country.

He came not to praise Eric Cantor, but to bash him.

Guitierrez was the lead speaker at a rally held by pro-amnesty group Casa de Virginia on the steps of the State Capitol, addressing a crowd amid signs reading "Eric Cantor: the one man blocking immigration reform" and "Eric Cantor, give us a vote!" He proclaimed: "We're here because the majority leader, Eric Cantor, controls the agenda of the Congress of the United States. And we have come here to say . . . stop being an obstacle; stop being in the way."

Asked by reporters about the timing of his visit, he replied that though some "might think we're here because there's a primary next week, nothing could be further from the truth."

And—yes—he managed to say it with a straight face.

Gutierrez's actual concern, like that of other amnesty fans, was the possibility, remote as it still seemed, that Eric Cantor might lose. Because if that happened, it would effectively kill the "compromise" immigration reform bill Cantor was vigorously pushing.

Veteran bull slinger that he is, Cantor played his part to the hilt. He immediately seized on Gutierrez's "attacks" as proof of his anti-immigration bona fides. "Just yesterday," his campaign proclaimed, "a liberal pro-amnesty group held a rally and encouraged their supporters to vote in our election for our opponent because Congressman Cantor is standing up to Obama on illegal immigration."

Cantor followed up by using a brief phone call with Obama as an excuse to put out a press release ripping the president on immigration. For the record, Obama denied they had even discussed immigration in the call. Since they both are practiced liars of long standing, it's impossible to know who, if either, was telling the truth.

As naked political maneuvering goes, this was about as cynical as it gets—and just about as obvious. But not to the geniuses of the press. Though a few conservative outlets joined Dave in calling Cantor on the deception—*Hot Air* web site headlined its piece "Democratic amnesty fan Luis Gutierrez helping Eric Cantor get reelected in order to protect immigration reform"—the charade fooled most in the mainstream press, including those at the influential *Richmond Times-Dispatch*, which dismissed our claims as the usual ravings of paranoid right-wing conspiracy theorists.

But in the end, like so many of the other stunts they had pulled, Cantor and Ray Allen's too-slick maneuver would prove disastrous. For among those who saw it for what it was, was the redoubtable Laura Ingraham. The two congressmen were, she acidly observed, "joined at the hip, working together, in a bipartisan fashion indeed, for the goal of immigration reform."

On Sunday, June 1, out of the blue, Laura Ingraham's staff informed us that she would be willing to come to the district and that we should set a rally for two days later—June 3, a week to the day before the primary.

Instantly, we went into overdrive, scrambling to find a venue. There was an hour or so of panic; since it was Sunday, everything was closed, and multiple calls went unanswered. Then we got word from one of our supporters that the Dominion Country Club might be available.

Fantastic venue—not only smack in the middle of Eric Cantor's neighborhood, but the very country club Cantor belongs to.

We blasted out the details of the rally on social media, sent dozens of emails, and robocalled every conservative voter in the district. We put Paul Revere to shame with cries of: "Laura Ingraham is coming! Laura Ingraham is coming!"

Still, by Tuesday we had no idea how many people would show, and an hour before the scheduled 6:00 p.m. start time, we began freaking out, because *nobody* was there. Laura arrived, looked around at the big, empty auditorium, and said: "Please tell me I didn't come down here for twenty people."

No worries. All at once, like the parting of the Red Sea, the floodgates opened. People started pouring in, and they didn't stop coming through the entire event. It was like they were falling from the sky. The parking lot adjacent to the venue, empty twenty minutes earlier, was completely packed, and so were both sides of the long drive leading toward it. People were parking literally three-quarters of a mile away, in Eric Cantor's neighborhood—in fact, *in front of Cantor's house.*

Game changer   *Richmond.com*

By 7:00, so many people were jamming the place that we had begun calculating: If each of them could get just ten people to the polls, we'd win by twenty points!

Laura was everything we hoped for. Beginning with a riff on that day's leading news event—saying that instead of trading five Taliban leaders for deserter Bowe Bergdahl, Obama should have traded Eric Cantor—she got straight to the point. When asked why she had come down to Richmond to campaign in a congressional district, she said: "Here's my answer: Because we're slowly losing our country. Because the Establishment has had its way election cycle after election cycle and kicked the electorate to the curb—sold out our values, misrepresented our views, looked down upon the very people who sent them to office—and then expect us to applaud them and send them back to office." Then she went after Cantor *hard* on immigration.

Dave was up next. Alternately genial and passionate, in his speech he touched not just on the Big Three issues that were converting so many voters—amnesty, Obamacare, and debt—but also on the IRS's targeting of conservatives, media bias, and, most important, Eric Cantor's fundamental dishonesty.

Ron Hedlund, up in the balcony, later reported that as he watched certain longtime Cantor supporters whom he knew had only been drawn by Laura, he could tell from the way they listened and responded that he was witnessing their transformation into Dave Brat supporters.

That was the magic of Ingraham's appearance. Cantor's commercials had been so ubiquitous that many Seventh District Republicans believed that there had to be *something* to Cantor's claim. Even if Dave was not exactly a *liberal*—as the ads so insistently maintained—surely the incumbent was the more solid conservative in the race.

So now the appearance of this renowned and unflinching conservative on Dave Brat's behalf was the very definition of cognitive dissonance for longtime Eric Cantor supporters. The grenade Cantor was holding, hoping it would not detonate before June 10, had exploded, blowing Cantor's campaign narrative to smithereens. The inevitable conclusion was that Cantor simply doesn't tell the truth. About anything.

We heard later there were many calls to Cantor's office that week, asking, "What's the deal with that liberal professor line?" or—from Cantor's perspective, more ominously—"Did the congressman really vote to fully fund Obamacare?"

By our calculations, Laura Ingraham's visit flipped the polls by as many as 10 points. It remains an open question whether we'd have won without it.

ZACH'S TAKE

As soon as she arrived, Laura Ingraham took one look at me and said, "You need a new suit."

She said it kindly, and she wasn't wrong. That suit was filthy, because I wore it all the time. It was ill-fitting, because by then I'd lost a bunch of weight. And this was even before she noticed the rip in the front of my pants, cleverly hidden beneath my jacket, from the month before when I was moving a chair out of my truck for the empty chair debate. Plus, by then I had a pretty nice beard going, and my hair was out of control–it took half a jar of pomade every day just to somewhat hold it down. I basically looked like a disheveled hobo.

However we got along great. I knew she had attended Dartmouth College, which was founded by my great, great-something grandfather, Eleazar Wheelock, so I brought that up. And before long we were singing this old Dartmouth drinking song about Eleazar:

Oh, Eleazar Wheelock was a very pious man;

He went into the wilderness to teach the IN-DI-AN

With a Gradus ad Parnassum, a Bible and a drum,

And five hundred gallons of New England rum.

Fill the bowl up! Fill the bowl up!

Drink to Eleazar,

And his primitive Alcazar,

Where he mixed drinks for the heathen in the goodness of his soul.

It was a terrific start to what might have been the most important evening of the whole campaign.

That's why it was so disheartening—though I guess not surprising—that in its coverage of the event, the *Richmond Times-Dispatch* focused on an innocuous off-script anti-Obama joke told by the man who introduced her. Here they were, with this huge story right in front of them—really, a major turning point in the campaign—and they totally missed it.

I did get a new suit, by the way—after we won. I was having coffee with the producer for *CBS This Morning*, a lovely woman named Jenna Gibson, and she said to me: "Before we put you on TV, you have to get a haircut, you have to get a new suit, and you have to shave that beard." I did all those things, and for the first time in months, I actually looked presentable. Though, regrettably, the lovely bartender at the local Irish pub no longer recognized me.

FOURTEEN

CANTOR'S POLLSTER
MISSES (BY 34 POINTS)

H ere's the question: Did the Cantor campaign believe their own hype? In the days leading up to the election, did they have any idea of the tsunami barreling their way?

For what it's worth, Cantor says absolutely not, telling ABC's John Karl a few days after the vote that he was "shocked" by the result. Then again, a hundred neuroscientists could devote their careers to studying Cantor and Allen's brains and never be able to tell when either was telling the truth.

It would be nice to think that, in fact, Cantor was increasingly desperate, that for once in his life he was sweating bullets. Just a few days before the election, a pleasant rumor had it that his mother was frantically calling her friends, urging them to come out and work the polls on little Eric's behalf. And local radio personality Jim Herring later told us that he heard from Cantor personally, asking him to work the polls. To which Jim replied—just before Cantor slammed down the phone—"Eric, I'm not even *voting* for you."

But there's also plenty of other evidence, notably Cantor's behavior during the month leading up to the primary, that if he indeed did have an inkling, he didn't pay it much attention.

Since the signs of what was afoot were so apparent to those on our side, this may strain credulity. But Cantor and company were focused on a completely different data set, less on the district and its voters—with whom they generally preferred to avoid too-intimate contact—than on the larger trends. Specifically, it was common wisdom in his circle of Establishment politicos, mainstream journalists, and others among the general run of Washington's smugly lobotomized that the Tea Party was finished. Or, as CNN headlined on May 21, with even greater finality, "Dead." This was the day after grassroots primary challengers to establishment incumbents went down in flames across the country. The one who got the most attention was Matt Bevin in Kentucky, whom Senate Majority Leader Mitch McConnell wiped out by a staggering 60 to 35.7 percent, but GOP insurgents lost almost as badly in Georgia, Pennsylvania, Idaho, and Oregon; and House Speaker John Boehner, McConnell's opposite number in the House, whom Cantor had every expectation of succeeding, had wiped out a pair of Tea Party challengers two weeks earlier, winning 69 percent of the vote. In the unlikely event the Cantor team wanted further reassurance, almost every one of those failed challengers had been overwhelmingly better funded than we were.

Worried? Though the district was little more than an hour away—fifteen minutes by helicopter—Cantor scarcely even bothered campaigning in person. He ran for reelection from the floor of the House, as majority leader. In that role, he pronounced (and made headlines) on every controversy, crisis, and piece of legislation then in the news—the VA scandal, sex trafficking, proposed new EPA regulations, even the Middle East—and appeared for multiple press availabilities with the rest of the leadership on the Capitol steps while all but ignoring the race and, more importantly, his district.

Majority Leader Eric Cantor did not deign to attack, or even speak of Dave Brat, content to let his dishonest ads back home do the dirty work. Instead, he focused his fire on those whose stature equaled his own: "Leader Cantor: Mr. President, Join Us in Helping America Work Again," read a typical news release from his office in response to the first-quarter GDP numbers:

"We have been here week in and week out and the House is working. We are trying to focus on getting people back to work. We are trying to focus on an America that works with solutions. Over 200 bills are still sitting in the Senate, many of them are bipartisan bills, some of them have Democratic lead sponsors, but yet Harry Reid and the Democratically controlled Senate refuse to take them up. This is outrageous that the Senate refuses to act; refuses to do constructive things that help get America working again . . ."

The calculation (if doing what came naturally even involved enough thought to merit such a designation) was that the peons in the Seventh District were permanently in his thrall, delighted and proud to have such an eminence representing them. His real constituency was his GOP House colleagues—the ones he expected to very soon elect him speaker. These (and especially those with IOUs in his back pocket) treated him with enormous respect and deference, if not always affection. And if any inquired about his forthcoming primary, Cantor reportedly always brushed it off as a nonissue, assuring them there was nothing to worry about.

A telling detail: The one trip Cantor took far from D.C. during this period was to Colorado, to campaign for *other people*—embattled Republican representatives Doug Lamborn of Colorado Springs and Mike Coffman of Aurora. (He also cohosted a fundraiser for New Mexico governor Susana Martinez, but that was from the comfort of his hometown—Washington, D.C.)

From all appearances, it was business as usual for Eric Cantor. Pausing only to pick up endorsements—the latest from the American Chemistry Council, many of whose blue-chip companies do business with the government, and which tossed in a $300,000 donation—he doggedly went about the nation's business. Dave Brat? Even as he was nudging Cantor's career toward the precipice, he was beneath the majority leader's notice.

And confirming that view were the polls. The surveys commissioned by Cantor's team had shown from the outset that he was far, far ahead—as, indeed, had ours . . . at first.

For it also depended upon how you read them. The raw data may not have looked terrific for us, but we'd been looking for a steady upward trajectory, and by the end, there was no doubt in our minds that we were surging. Our final internal poll—this time not a push poll, intended to sway voters, but looking for a clear-eyed state of the race—showed us down by just 39-46, with 16 percent undecided. More, the calling was done on June 2, a day *before* Laura Ingraham's appearance on Dave's behalf.

BRAT—GOTV Poll—0602		
Call Progress		
Live Person:	2,808	65%
Answering Machine:	655	15%
Fax:	38	1%
Busy:	42	1%
No Answer:	185	4%
Problem:	589	14%
Total:	4,317	

Q1: Planning to vote on June 10?		
1: Yes	427	79%
2: No	65	12%
3: Undecided	49	9%
Total:	541	

Q2: Would you vote for Brat, or Cantor?		
1: Brat	187	39%
2: Cantor	221	46%
3: Undecided	75	16%
Total:	483	

Q3: What is your gender?		
1: Male	171	38%
2: Female	285	63%
Total:	456	

Q4: What is your age?		
1: 18–30 years old	14	3%
2: 31–39 years old	11	3%

3: 40–49 years old	29	7%
4: 50–59 years old	75	17%
5: 60 or over	310	71%
Total:	439	

Even better, another poll, commissioned by the conservative site the *Daily Caller* and so presumably neutral, was released the same day. Conducted by Vox Populi Polling, based on interviews with "583 active primary voters," it, too, showed the Brat campaign surging, if not to the degree indicated by ours. Combining those firmly in support of each of the candidates with those listed as leaning, it had Cantor at 52 and Brat at 40. The web site trumpeted it as a "Shock Poll!"

It is possible, even likely, that at this moment Cantor's brain trust was at least the *tiiiiniest* bit concerned, because it hardly seems coincidental that a couple days later the Cantor campaign leaked their own internal polling numbers; ones that if taken to heart might well have dampened the enthusiasm of our people and depressed the vote.

It was all there on Friday, June 6, in the *Washington Post*: Cantor internal poll claims 34-point lead over primary opponent Brat.

The story reported that according to a "survey of 400 likely Republican primary voters" conducted by Cantor pollster John McLaughlin of McLaughlin & Associates and carrying a margin of error of ±4.9 percentage points, Cantor was cruising to victory with a "62 percent to 28 percent lead over Brat, an economics professor running to Cantor's right," with 11 percent undecided.

It later emerged that the Cantor campaign had paid $75,000 for the poll, which not only failed to demoralize our people, but ended up turning pollster McLaughlin into a national joke. As a typical post-election Twitter comment observed, "Eric Cantor's pollster got it wrong by more than 34 percent. This is what happens when you don't fund math and science." With the World Cup just around the corner, others guessed at McLaughlin's soccer predictions: "Eric Cantor's pollster says Belgium will definitely win the World Cup, beating Honduras 17–0 in the final." "Just checked with Eric Cantor's internal pollster, and I'm betting a kidney on the U.S. winning the World Cup."

Did Cantor and Allen really believe they'd win by 34 points? Perhaps not. But they surely believed they'd win—and that if it was by anything less than twenty, it would be an embarrassment. Their major miscalculation was in focusing their polling on those who had consistently voted in past Republican primaries. In doing so, they missed all the new voters—the conservatives long put off by politics as usual—we were working so hard to turn out.

But there was no question in their minds that Cantor *would* win. Easily. As he always had, both by virtue of his stature and because his opponent had been buried so deep beneath an avalanche of advertising that he'd never be heard from again, politically or otherwise.

Talk about a sure thing! By the end of the campaign, there had been *seventeen* different Cantor mail pieces sent out, each lavishly produced and sporting a fully tested message and slogan designed for maximum effect. How could anyone guess that they would all be overshadowed by a single, far simpler, piece we mailed out the final week? It featured a picture of Dave Brat against a blue background and read "Don't Believe the Lies. You Have a Conservative Choice on June 10." On the back was a list of Eric Cantor's biggest lies: the truth in plain English, with citations to boot.

In the outside world, ignorant of the dynamics of the race, it was still universally expected that the House majority leader and soon-to-be speaker would breeze to victory against his unknown and underfunded upstart of an opponent. But by the last Sunday, two days before the vote, we knew what was coming. Our door-knockers had come back to the office late that afternoon, all with variations on the same theme: Almost every single voter they'd talked to would be voting for Dave Brat. Some also reported that lots of people not on our list of voters had spotted their Dave Brat T-shirts and volunteered, "We are voting for your guy!"

That evening, we got a call from John Fredericks, one of the few media people who'd been supportive throughout. He was wondering whether he should bother showing up to cover election night. After all, as far as most of the world was concerned, it was a done deal. Did we have any shot at all of winning this thing?

Come, we told him: "We're gonna win."

"Are you shitting me?" he asked. "How much are you going to win by?"

"Nine points."

Who could have guessed that estimate would be low?

FIFTEEN

OUR LONGEST DAY

" Irene and I had been going nonstop for weeks, and we were pretty beat," recalls Pete Churins, "so that Monday before the election, we were at home, just taking a little break. But it's like I was a rabid dog. I suddenly stand up and say: 'C'mon, Irene—we gotta go hit some more doors!' Man, we just couldn't stop, not when we were so close. This thing was too important."

Allen Wagner, another of our most faithful volunteers, had been making phone calls in the office every single day since the end of March, sitting at the front desk, checking in volunteers, calling registered voters, doing whatever was asked of him. No days off and no pay.

And people still wonder why we won.

At that point, other campaigns would have been focusing on locking down their voters and making sure that they got to the polls, but our volunteers were still going all-out throughout the district, trying to unearth new voters.

We had two win scenarios. One was extremely low turnout. That favored us, because it meant only the most motivated voters were turning out—and we had the most motivated voters. The other was extremely high turnout: a tidal wave of frustrated, fed-up and long alienated voters, the ultimate vindication of our door knocking strategy. The only way we'd lose is if the primary was dominated by the usual suspects, voters who turned out less by conviction than by habit, the ones who'd reelected Eric Cantor cycle after cycle. Too many older voters would be especially bad news—both because historically their minds are toughest to change and because of the small fortune Cantor had spent lying to them about Dave's eagerness to take away their Social Security. Besides, we knew from our data that they skewed heavily toward Cantor.

The crucial last step was making sure we had a strong presence at the polls. This would be our final—and for some voters, our first— chance to draw the contrast between Dave and Cantor. Incredible as it seemed to those of us living inside the bubble of the campaign (and, given what it showed about the nation's political life and culture, as disheartening), lots of voters would be heading off to the polls undecided—which is to say still persuadable.

Getting our Primary Day operation in place meant committing several hundred volunteers to the task and, of particular importance in a district that ran from blue-collar Tea Party to old line Virginia aristocratic, matching the right ones with the right precincts. Then, too, they had to be briefed, delivered the necessary materials, and kept fed and watered from the opening of the polls at 6 a.m. until their closing at 7 p.m. It was itself a minor military operation—our Longest Day, the decisive battle in a long and grueling war—and we wanted to be prepared for all eventualities. If we were going to blow it now, it wasn't going to be for lack of effort.

There are 227 polling places scattered throughout the nine counties and parts of the city of Richmond that make up the Seventh District. We had prioritized them by importance, dispersing our forces accordingly.

Our primary focus was on the district's population centers, the counties of Hanover, Henrico, and Chesterfield, which together account for three-quarters of the district's residents. We were most confident about Hanover, Virginia's most Republican county, where Kim Singhas was commander-in-chief, along with her partners in crime Dale Taylor, Daryl Carr, and Steve Tetrault. Indeed, from the outset of the campaign, knowing that Kim had things covered, we'd hardly had to give Hanover a second thought. The campaign would have a presence at each of the county's thirty-six polling locations, and throughout the day, a cadre of Hanover homeschoolers would be making calls—and, if necessary, follow-up calls—from the campaign office to district residents pegged as Brat voters.

We also felt good about Henrico, both Cantor and Dave's home county, where our operation was spearheaded by Anita and Mark Hile's Henrico Tea Party. In the last week, the door knockers working in the precincts we'd targeted within Henrico County were receiving a fantastic reaction—with seven, eight, even nine of every ten voters saying they were for Dave. Even if a third of them were lying, we would still be okay.

Chesterfield was more of a wild card. In allocating resources, we'd been somewhat hands-off in Chesterfield, leaving the heaviest lifting to Ken Davis, the county coordinator—himself a wild card; while Ken had proven himself one helluva great radio pitchman, we hadn't had enough feedback from the field to guess with any precision how effectively our organization would perform in the county. Ken told us to trust him, and we had no choice but to believe him.

Suzanne Ircink had been working around the clock in Spotsylvania County, so we were reasonably confident that we would be all right there, although we did not have enough data to make a reliable prediction.

Dewey and Janet McDonnell, conservative stalwarts, were our coordinators in Culpeper. Dewey and Janet know the area like the back of their hands. This was not their first rodeo: They had worked to elect several conservative candidates and had engineered the takeover of the local Republican Party by the Tea Party. Dewey said that they were where they wanted to be headed into the last week, but we knew that we had not hit as many doors as we would have liked. Still, we had to trust them and hope for the best.

We expected that our weakest counties would be Culpeper and Orange, rural areas not conducive to door knocking. Still, though neither county was likely to draw more than a few thousand voters, even here we made sure to staff the larger polling places.

Over the duration of the campaign, we had, of course, run the numbers hundreds of times. There was paper all over the office covered with calculations and projections, all of them aimed at adding up to 50 percent plus 1 (plus a couple thousand more—which is to say enough to win a rigged recount). We ran the numbers in our heads as we drifted off to sleep, and we ran them again as soon as we woke up. Would we take Chesterfield? Was Henrico as strong as it looked? Okay, no doubt at all we'd win Hanover—but by how much? If Cantor broke even close to even in Hanover, our strongest county, the one we'd worked more thoroughly than any other, we were in *huge* trouble.

Indeed, the first reports out of Hanover would probably tell the tale.

Fittingly, for the final act, the contrast with the Cantor operation was as striking as ever. At innumerable polling places, including some of the district's most important precincts, Cantor's people were all but invisible. Zero people handing out Cantor literature and expressing—or at least pretending to express—enthusiasm for the majority leader. Those who were there were the usual paid "volunteers," most of whom couldn't have cared less.

Ron Hedlund, working a precinct at Hungary Creek Middle School (which would end up recording the fourth-largest turnout of the sixty-six in crucial Henrico), reports that our poll workers found just one lonely Cantor "volunteer" on the scene:

"After a while, we got to chatting, and he was a nice young man, but he had no clue what Eric Cantor stood for. He'd been bused in from northern Virginia, and basically he just sat off to the side by himself—never engaged voters, unless somebody saw his Cantor shirt and approached him. Just no passion at all. Actually, he was very conservative, and I told him, 'Boy, it sounds like if you lived in the district, you'd definitely be a Dave Brat guy.' Meanwhile, I was getting voters as they came in and was turning some of them and even talking to them on the way out, just trying to figure out how the vote was going."

Throughout the day, one of us – Gray – worked the polls, while the other – Zach – remained in the campaign office, managing the phone callers and trying to get a feel from everyone in the field. It was the same in precinct after precinct, county after county. Our volunteers were so well prepared and so passionate, they reported flipping people left and right all day long. Often it wasn't even all that difficult, since they were already with us but just didn't know it. Until then, for all our efforts, most of what they knew had come from Cantor's ads. But now, with a copy of the famous Cantor–Brat issues comparison sheet in hand, a couple of minutes to consider it, and someone eager to answer their questions, they walked in, voted for Dave, and thanked us on the way out.

It was truly amazing; after all these years representing the Seventh District, Eric Cantor simply inspired no loyalty or enthusiasm. Heaven knows there are few in the world less deserving of sympathy, but it was almost enough to make you feel sorry for the guy. Almost.

How disconnected was Cantor from the district? How's this? He didn't even bother coming back to vote—the absentee congress-man voted by *absentee ballot*. That morning, even as Dave Brat was greeting voters at the biggest precinct in the district, Eric Cantor was in Washington, D.C., holding a fundraiser with lobbyists at a Capitol Hill Starbucks.

The next day, another fact would be widely circulated, to much ridicule: In the course of outspending our campaign by more than forty to one, the Cantor campaign spent more than $168,000 on steak dinners alone.

Sympathy? Heck, if ever there was a corrupt, self-serving pol who had it coming . . .

Back at our campaign headquarters, the atmosphere was electric. Everyone who was not out working the polls was pumped, sensing what was coming even as we were reluctant to say it out loud. The county coordinators were checking in regularly, and we were also hearing from others in the field—as well as checking out various precincts ourselves, constantly trying to get a feel for what was going on. What we were seeing looked good: pretty brisk turnout across the district. But we tried not to be too persuaded by that. There are tea leaves to be read all over the place on any election day, along with anecdotes that can set your spirits soaring—or send them crashing down to earth. The wise course is to stay as calm as possible and await the results.

But who's kidding whom? We yo-yoed back and forth along with everyone else. And for all the encouraging signs, there were also occasional worrisome ones.

Without question, the day's worst moment came mid-morning, when the normally imperturbable Kim called in, reporting that a large number of senior citizens were turning out in her precinct in Hanover. "I was really worried about that," she said later. "If someone's going to vote for your guy, they'll usually give you some indication—smile, give a thumbs-up, or say, 'Hey, you got my vote.' But most of these people didn't stop or chat at our table or really give us any encouragement at all. I believed they were long time Cantor voters—hard-line Republicans."

Then, in mid-afternoon, around 3:00, she noticed an unmistakable shift at her precinct. All at once it was "guys in pickup trucks with the ladders and the toolboxes on the trucks pouring in to vote. Western Hanover is pretty rural, and they'd probably hauled out at six in the morning traveling to get to a job, so they couldn't vote early. But they were here now, and my line to every one of them who pulled up in a pickup truck was 'Eric Cantor supports amnesty. That's 14 million lost jobs for American workers.'"

But these voters didn't have to be sold. Most of them had heard our radio ads and read our literature, and they knew all about Dave and—just as important—about the yawning chasm between what Cantor said and what he did.

Soon Kim was totally feeling it. "This is looking really good now," she reported. "They're flooding into the polling place by the dozens."

And she was right. Dave won every precinct in Hanover County—all thirty-six of them—many by a two-to-one margin over Cantor.

As it would turn out, this was largely the pattern everywhere: quick early, dead before lunch, high elderly turnout midday, another slowdown, then an explosion of middle-aged working-class voters from 4 to 7.

Turnout was as big as we'd hoped. The door knocking had vastly expanded the Seventh's electoral universe!

Our candidate could see it, too. By late afternoon, Dave's spirits couldn't have been higher. He was campaigning outside the Tuckahoe precinct, arguably the largest and most important precinct in the district. Lots of people, as soon as they saw him, were giving him a thumbs-up, or slapping his back, and telling him he had their vote.

One of Cantor's "volunteers" was out there at the same time—a gentleman named John O'Bannon, a member of the House of Delegates and a peripheral part of the Cantor–Ray Allen machine—and he could hardly believe what he was seeing. He was actually working hard, hustling after voters, but he was getting the opposite reaction. Again and again he'd thrust out his hand and say: "Thank you for coming out, I hope you'll give Congressman Cantor your support"—and the voter wouldn't respond or maybe just nod noncommittally and keep walking. Then the same voter would come to Dave, who'd say, "Hi, I'm Dave Brat. If you think Washington's broken, I need your support to help fix it." And more times than not, the voter stopped and they'd start talking about the issues, or maybe the charges Cantor had made, and very quickly Dave would bring the voter around. He was personally flipping people left and right.

Watching it happen, O'Bannon was dumbstruck. This was *Cantor's* home turf, *his* people, home to the "country club elite." If there was one precinct where Cantor should be absolutely creaming us, they were standing in it!

Finally O'Bannon had to acknowledge the obvious. "Looks like you're doing pretty well, Dave," he offered.

Dave nodded. "Yeah—I really think we're gonna pull this off."

"No way," O'Bannon scoffed. "Not according to the polling I'm seeing. The response you're getting right now, it's just because you're here. It's not happening anywhere else."

"Fine—okay," said Dave. "Guess we'll see."

Right until the bitter end, they never saw it coming. They thought that not only would they win, but win easily. No other outcome was conceivable. Though they may have lived and worked in the district, having drunk the Kool-Aid, they were as arrogant and clueless as the national press—which is about as arrogant and clueless as you can get.

Not to sound petty—but that made it all the sweeter.

SIXTEEN

Duane Berger

The polls closed at 7 p.m., and thanks to the lightning-fast Opti-Scan tabulators being used in the district, the first result came in at 7:04. The call was from Sally Fritzsche, at Hanover's

Rural Point precinct, and she was breathless: "You won't believe this! Brat 303, Cantor 142!"

It took an instant to register. "303 to 142?" More than two-thirds of the vote, and in a bellweather district! A district that in the last election went to Cantor two-to-one! This was beyond incredible! If the margins in the rest of Hanover turned out to be anything like this . . .

But already other calls were pouring in.

Staples Mills in Henrico: Brat 412, Cantor 254. Boom!

Shenandoah in Chesterfield, a classic swing precinct: Brat 241, Cantor 140. Boom!

It was beyond unbelievable. So in those first moments, we hesitated to let ourselves completely believe it. Steven Mond, our volunteer technological and data guru, usually so reserved he never spoke an unnecessary word, had developed his own algorithm to evaluate the returns and suddenly, five minutes in, he got up from his computer and started running around the room, screaming, "We've won! We've won!"

"Shut up, Steve!" we shouted at once. "STOP IT! IT'S NOT OVER 'TIL IT'S OVER!"

Yet at the same time, it was impossible not to think "My gosh, if *Steve Mond* is saying it, it's *gotta* be real!"

Everything coming in said we were blowing it out of the water, especially in the precincts where we'd worked to turn out fed-up voters who normally sit out Republican primaries. In Henrico and Chesterfield, they'd turned out in droves.

Now the New Kent districts were coming in:

Quinton: Brat 195, Cantor 122. Boom.

Southern Branch: Brat 224, Cantor 96. BOOM!

In fact, ten of eleven New Kent precincts were going our way, en route to our winning the county 63 to 37. (Thank you, Pete, Irene and Matt!)

Though it seemed hours, it was more like fifteen minutes, but now even we were ready to believe. Our two-pronged strategy had worked to perfection. The final numbers would show that primary turnout had increased over 2012 by a massive 19,000, or 28 percent—yet Cantor's total had *decreased* by nearly 8,500 votes.

The result: Brat 36,105, Cantor 28,912—or 55.53 to 44.47 percent.

More than *eleven points*.

Give Cantor his due: he did manage to hold Tuckahoe—by all of twenty-one votes, and then only because Dave hadn't shown up to start flipping voters until late in the afternoon. John O'Bannon is probably still trying to figure out what happened.

As the magnitude of what was happening began to sink in, there were a few moments of wild exultation—and then, abruptly, one last spasm of doubt. Or paranoia. Or a three-week caffeine binge coming home to roost. Or just the residue of bitter, hard-earned experience. Whatever it was, suddenly we were seized by the thought that Ray Allen would find some way to steal the election!

So we grabbed Ron, and...wait, let's let him tell it:

> Suddenly Zach starts freaking out, yelling that I need to get down to the state board of elections. So I start

speeding downtown in my truck, wondering what I'm gonna do when I get there to keep Ray from stealing it. Is there even a way? Well, fortunately the numbers for us were just too big. I'm listening to the radio, and before I even get there, they call it for Dave. Nothing to do but turn around and head straight to the party.

Duane Berger

Yet while we in the Seventh knew it was all over, the rest of the country was still in the dark; even now, the mainstream media maintained almost total silence. It was as if the information flooding into the nation's media centers was so preposterous it couldn't be believed.

Flipping through the channels, we waited to see: Who would be the first to break from the herd?

Surprisingly, it was CNN. Around 7:30, one of their producers called the office, shell-shocked: "It looks like you guys actually won."

"Damn straight!"

Within moments there was mayhem, and the calls were flooding in by the dozen, then the score. Fox and Friends, Face the Nation, Greta, NBC Nightly News—you name the show, their producer was calling. We'd never had any dealings with any of these shows before; how on earth did they even have our cell numbers? Was there some file they'd kept during all those months when we were pleading for coverage and no one would answer our calls?

Now they're interested   *Duane Berger*

Now the scramble for access to Dave Brat was ruthless. The camera trucks were doing 150 heading south to Richmond from D.C. on I-95, and producers were *demanding* that he be made available—NOW!

"Uh-uh, sorry. Not possible."

In other words: Screw you!

There was a time we'd actually looked up to network news people—the national network reporters and Wolf Blitzers of the world, the Sunday morning anchors and the print reporters from the brand-name papers. But, having experienced them up close and personal their smug self-certainty and how readily they twisted the "facts" to conform to whatever narrative they were pushing, we were no longer under any illusions. So now here they were, having totally missed the story, finally ready to give Dave Brat and his campaign meaningful coverage—because it was in their interest.

Too late. Shoe, meet other foot. Now *we* didn't need *them*.

Of course, it was another story when it came to those who had been there when it counted: Laura Ingraham and Mark Levin among the national heavyweights; Doc Thompson from the *Blaze*; radio hosts Joe Thomas and Rob Schilling out of Charlottesville. And we also made a few minutes for Jake Sherman of *Politico*, about the only mainstream reporter outside the district who'd given the race any coverage at all.

Even though Fox had been as MIA (and as certain of a Cantor blowout) as everyone else, Dave appeared that evening on Sean Hannity's show. Of the approximately 260 media outlets begging for Dave that evening, we went with Sean because (a) there was no better platform to reach the millions nationwide who were as excited and heartened by the night's results as we were and (b) his young producer was by far the most attractive and charming of all those doing the asking.

And—oh, yes, we also agreed that he would do a brief spot early the next morning with NBC's Chuck Todd. This was a thank-you to Todd for having done a brief but quite friendly last-minute interview with Dave on Primary Day morning. Big mistake. We naively assumed that this appearance would be equally innocuous, with Todd simply offering congratulations. But now that Dave Brat was the Republican nominee, the reporter went after him full-bore, trying to trip up an exhausted Dave on a range of policy issues.

Lesson learned: No matter how pleasant they seem, they are *all* snakes in the grass.

Needless to say, it was something other than a surprise that in the following days, the media "analysis" of Dave's victory (or, more precisely, Cantor's loss) would often be comically off base. One major storyline had it that we'd been greatly helped by Virginia's lack of party registration and open primary system, enabling us to turn out a massive number of Democrats for Dave. "There was a major outreach to Democrats in that district," Larry Sabato, director of the University of Virginia Center for Politics, told CNN. "You had Brat operatives going to Democratic Party committees, even on election eve, asking them to go to the polls to get rid of Eric Cantor. It had nothing to do with Dave Brat. There were robocalls to Democrats in that district, wanting—telling—Democrats to come out to the polls."

While a humiliated Ray Allen—and his hapless pollster—eagerly seized upon the claim, it was way off base. There was no outreach by the campaign to Democrats, who saw this election for what it was—a Republican fight—and it showed at the polls. Turnout was light in traditionally Democrat precincts and extremely heavy in those that vote Republican. Indeed, we estimated that Democrats constituted no more than three to five percent of primary voters—which means they made no practical difference at all; while it's likely they skewed our way, even if every one had gone for Cantor, we still would have won going away.

Then, too, as day follows night, given Dave's strong reliance on Tea Party support, came the charge that the results had been influenced by racism—in this case, the fact that Cantor is Jewish. Is it even necessary to point out that Cantor had been elected in the same district, by the same voters, in *ten* prior elections? But why bother? There's no arguing with the vile souls of the left desperate to confirm their own ugly prejudices and survive by propagating such poison.

Then there were the stories that discounted immigration as a major factor in the race, lest other Republicans move to the right on the issue to avoid Cantor's fate—and still other stories that mistakenly argued immigration was the *only* issue.

It's not as if the real reasons were all that hard to fathom—they were right there in what Dave had been saying for months: yes, about immigration, but also about free markets and crony capitalism, adherence to the Republican Creed and ethical behavior in the public sphere. All any reporter would have had to do was spend sixty seconds listening to Ken Davis's radio ad or talk to any of the hundreds of volunteers celebrating with us that night.

In fact, we billed the gathering not as a victory party, but as a "Grassroots Celebration" for the volunteers, and it was a total blast. People were out of their minds with joy—hugging, crying. Even people who despised each other (and, like most campaigns, we had our fair share of those) were falling into each other's arms, declaring this the greatest moment of their lives. Both of us were hoisted into the air and carried about the room.

Even the venue reflected the spirit of our perpetually broke, never-say-die effort. Since there was no way we could have sprung for a hotel ballroom— not with every last cent going for last-minute radio spots—we held the party in the open foyer of an office building off Cox Road. Its chief virtue? Plenty of parking.

Of course there was a less pleasant aspect to the evening. What is it they say? "Success has a million fathers, failure is an orphan?" Well, in addition to the hundreds who'd genuinely made it happen, there were plenty of would-be dads sniffing around the party that evening, eager to talk themselves up to any reporter who'd listen, never mind that most had written us off when the going was rough. And then there were the grandees of the Republican Congressional Committee who hustled down to Richmond, wanting in on the action; never mind that hours earlier, they'd been all in for Cantor.

Dave himself, when he took to the podium, couldn't have been more ecstatic over "the miracle that just happened," declaring "it did not just float down from heaven" but was the result of "a lot of sweat and a lot of shoe leather . . . . it's about returning the country to constitutional principles; it's about returning the country to Judeo-Christian principles; it's about taking this country back to free market principles, where no one is favored." And he repeated, as he had for months, that he would continue to hold those ideals dear when he went to Congress.

The party went on past 2 a.m. and, busy with others, accepting congratulations (and more than a few drinks), the two of us did not sit down together until it was over. Then, exhausted and frazzled, we sat nursing beers, talking about our families. One of our moms had spent the entire day, 6 a.m. to 7 p.m., working the polls with a friend; the other had sent out a mock-desperate Facebook post earlier in the evening: "Zach, please call CNN. They won't stop bothering me!"

We soon fell silent, watching a replay of Cantor's concession speech on a TV in the corner. When the camera panned the audience in the elegant hotel ballroom, you could see that some of his staffers—people we'd run across repeatedly during the course of the campaign—looked close to tears. Heck, from their faces, you'd think three-quarters of the human race had just been wiped out in a nuclear explosion. We exchanged a smile, recalling how arrogant they'd often been—so contemptuous of our effort, so sure they were going to stomp us beyond recognition.

But the moment was also bittersweet. Dave had been most gracious tonight, singling the two of us out for credit, extending his appreciation for how we'd "worked eighteen-hour days when I was passed out and exhausted." Yet now that we'd crossed the finish line, we had a pretty good idea we'd be moving on.

Not that that was all bad. Here in the heavily Republican Seventh, winning the primary was tantamount to winning the general. Our job was done; the vultures from the National Republican Congressional Committee could take it from here. We'd already gotten word of another long shot race in the offing: a conservative businessman looking for a dedicated campaign team to knock off a liberal Democratic congressional incumbent.

We clinked glasses: "To victory."

A sip, and we clinked again: "To taking the country back, one race at a time."

AFTERMATH

A politician who stays true to his campaign promises? Impossible!

Yet since taking office in November 2014, Dave Brat has been exactly that. He has stood against the Republican leadership by voting (even on procedural votes) against Obama's executive order on immigration, against every vote on the Trans-Pacific Partnership, against crony capitalist programs like the Import–Export Bank, against Boehner's reelection as speaker, and against increased spending. Moreover, he has held over fifteen town halls in the Seventh District since taking office.

In short, he has been just the congressman we all hoped he would be.

Brutal honesty? At one town meeting in Richmond, discussing the Washington, D.C. cesspool that he's now observed up close and personal, Dave was characteristically blunt:

> There is only one party in Washington . . . . In ten years, every dime of federal revenue will be spent on entitlement spending—Medicaid, Medicare, Social Security, and Medicare Part D. There will be no money for the military, but the Republican leadership and Democrats do not care. They just care about lining their pockets and staying in power . . . . Big business and the lobbyists rule Washington. Ninety percent of your elected representatives do not care about the welfare of the country . . . . Boehner works with Pelosi and avoids the Freedom Caucus—conservatives—in order to get the votes to pass everything the Democrats want. One-party system.

This is called making all the right enemies. It's also known as character.

By way of contrast, there's Eric Cantor. Three months after the election, Cantor joined the investment bank Moelis with a starter package of $3.4 million.

Still, his defeat was a devastating body blow to the Establishment, all the more so because it was so totally unexpected. But did it change who they are or how they operate? Did it lessen their determination to maintain their stranglehold on the Republican Party?

Does a stake in the heart of one vampire spell the end of the whole species? Or even of *that* vampire? In this fight to reclaim America's soul, we can't afford to rest on our laurels for even a millisecond.

Proof? The following was published on January 17, 2014, just seven months after Eric Cantor went down in flames. And, as the *American Thinker* felt obligated to point out, it "appeared in the *Washington Post*, not the *Onion*."

> Cantor speaks to establishment Republicans in Va. about how to win
>
> Dave Brat's supporters feel shut out from meeting
>
> RICHMOND — Republican Eric Cantor on Saturday addressed the inaugural gathering of a group formed after grass-roots activists helped Dave Brat topple the former majority leader in last summer's GOP primary.
>
> The day-long meeting of the Virginia Conservative Network featured a who's who of establishment Republicans in the mold of Cantor . . . . According to organizers, Cantor gave an invitation-only crowd of more than 100 people tips on how to frame their message to voters as Republicans prepare to defend their slim majority in the state Senate this year. Activists from the establishment wing of the party are also focused on delivering the swing state of Virginia for the party's 2016 presidential nominee . . . . Cantor was joined by Linwood Cobb, his right-hand man in the Seventh District Republican Committee whose ouster foreshadowed Cantor's own defeat. Rep. Brat and his supporters were not invited."

Our friend Ron Hedlund often quotes Benjamin Franklin's reply when he was asked by Mrs. Elizabeth Powel at the close of the Constitutional Convention what kind of government the Framers had given us. Never has the great man's response been more apt than today: "A republic, madam, if you can keep it."

"Those who expect to reap the blessings of freedom, must like men, undergo the fatigue of supporting it."

-*Thomas Paine*

Preliminary Plan, Dave Brat for Congress Campaign

It is essential to have a short list of cohesive points around which an entire campaign can be built. These should be raised in every interview, every speech, and every meeting between now and Election Day.

We propose that Dave make the campaign predominantly about Eric Cantor, with his résumé as a backdrop to establish he is a viable candidate, qualified and ready to serve in Congress. He will defeat Cantor by proving that Cantor has lost touch with his constituents, intimidates his opponents, and is a crony capitalist. If these points are effectively portrayed, we can significantly raise his name ID, and he can win. The main task is to expose the real Eric Cantor.

Cantor will attempt to marginalize Dave by seeking to portray him as exclusively a Tea Party candidate. We absolutely need full Tea Party support (and must deserve it), but we also need to reach a wider audience.

Key Points

ONE: Eric Cantor is a consummate Washington insider who no longer works for his constituents.

- *Cantor has become inaccessible to his constituents. He did not host a town hall during the August recesses in 2012 and 2013 (he held just one private town hall in 2011). Constituents find it nearly impossible to make an appointment with him.*

- *Cantor no longer even reaches out to the Culpeper GOP to let them know when he is in town.*

- *He hosts only staged events at businesses that are either private events or not open to the press.*

- *Eric Cantor has created an us-versus-them atmosphere in the district. He has created a culture of intimidation where people are afraid to speak against him for fear of retribution. Business owners are afraid to speak out, as are political operatives who wish to continue a career in politics.*

- *When you are afraid of your congressman, you know that it is time to get rid of your congressman.*

TWO: Expose Eric Cantor's voting record.

a. *Time and time again, Cantor has voted for more spending. According to the CBO, interest payments, as a percentage of federal outlays, are expected to rise from the current 6.4 percent to 11.1 percent by 2018, 12.9 percent by 2020, and 14.7 percent by 2024. These projections assume annual growth at between 3 and 4 percent, which is above the 2 to 3 percent growth we have experienced in the last several years. We are not talking about twenty or thirty years down the road; we are talking about four years from now. If we do not correct this trajectory, then there are going to be dramatic consequences. It is not time to be worried about the image of the Republican Party (which is already in the tank); it is time to lead and to save the Republic. It is now or never. A portable national debt clock should be on display at every event you attend.*

    b. Push back against Cantor's support of comprehensive immigration reform. According to a Harris poll, 81 percent of native-born citizens think the schools should teach students to be proud of being American. Only 50 percent of naturalized U.S. citizens do. While 67 percent of native-born Americans believe our Constitution is a higher legal authority than international law, only 37 percent of naturalized citizens agree. A Pew Research Center poll of all Hispanics, immigrant and citizen alike, found that Hispanics take a dimmer view of capitalism than even people who describe themselves as "liberal Democrats." While 47 percent of self-described "liberal Democrats" hold a negative view of capitalism, 55 percent of Hispanics do. Seventy-five percent of Hispanic immigrants and 55 percent of Asian immigrants support bigger government—also according to Pew. Even after three generations in America, Hispanics still support bigger government 55 percent to 36 percent, compared to the general public, which opposes bigger government 48 percent to 41 percent.

THREE: Stress Cantor's history as a crony capitalist.

    a. STOCK Act. Changed bill to allow family members of congressmen to continue to inside trade. Loophole makes bill worthless.

b. *Corporate welfare has been doled out in record numbers since Cantor has been in congress ($1.2 trillion since 2000). Cantor has failed to stand up against it.*

Throughout 2009, Cantor helped lead opposition to mortgage cram-down—a no-cost measure to help borrowers negotiate lower interest rates and avoid foreclosure. While Cantor marshaled opposition to these policies, he did not disclose that both his own wealth and his wife's were connected to the mortgage industry. Diane Cantor at the time worked as a managing director at New York Private Bank & Trust, a major mortgage bank and TARP recipient. In 2009, Eric Cantor also owned a portion of a family debt collection law firm. According to his personal finance disclosure, Cantor owned up to a $100,000 stake in Cantor & Cantor, the debt collection law firm run by his family.

Press Strategy

1. *Dave should leverage existing relationships with NBC 12 and other outlets (even if he appears in his role as Professor Brat).*

2. *He should take almost every invitation that is given.*

3. *To the extent possible, we should seek to take the campaign national.*

Grassroots Strategy

a. *We need to be knocking doors in huge numbers, as well as hitting all major events to hand out literature. All volunteers must be well educated in the principal campaign themes, as well as in Eric Cantor's liabilities. Door knocking, in this case, is not only about IDs, it is about persuasion. Volunteers must be able to cite immigration statistics (not just say that there is a rule of law, etc.). They must also take care not to unnecessarily alienate mainstream Republicans. For instance, should not say anything about impeaching Obama, Agenda 21, or anything of the sort. Even when these observations may be on target, they may be counterproductive.*

b. *We should attempt to broaden our reach by getting in front of as many organizations and associations in the district as possible, including Rotary Clubs, business organizations, and veterans groups. This will be useful in fighting against Cantor's attempt to marginalize Dave as just a Tea Party challenger.*

Fundraising

We should seek out personal meetings and meet-and-greets with influential figures in the business/country club community. In these meetings,

- *Cite the foregoing immigration statistics.*

- *Cite CBO statistics.*

- *Raise how Eric Cantor does not stand for free markets. It is not just about Cantor voting to raise the debt ceiling; he has also teamed up with Maxine Waters to water down basic reforms to the National Flood Insurance Program*

- *Voted for the most recent Farm Bill, in which Republicans gave up on decoupling food stamp reauthorizations to the rest of the farm bill*

- *Not stood for reforms to Medicare and Social Security*

- *Not taken a firm stand even on one token reform—for example, by demanding reducing the COLA on Social Security*

Social Security, Medicare, and Medicaid spending are set to double in the next ten years, yet Cantor stands idly by rather than address this dire threat to our long-term economic outlook. Eric Cantor never shows the willingness to take a stand, even on the most basic common-sense reform.

Staff

Lean and mean is the byword. Three or a maximum of four paid staffers, augmented by skilled and highly dedicated volunteers. Business owners and key Republican donors in the Richmond area will take note of the staff to determine the campaign's legitimacy. Staffers must fully believe in the candidate and the message, which should be reflected in performance: sixteen- and eighteen-hour workdays, if necessary. Cantor will use whatever ammunition—including staffers' backgrounds—to marginalize the campaign, so staffers must be rock-solid.

Acknowledgments

We have so many people to thank that it is difficult to even know where to begin. Dave Brat's race was not won by one person, two people, or even ten people. It was a group effort on the part of hundreds of extremely dedicated volunteers committed to restoring our country to greatness. It was humbling to see people give hundreds of hours of their time and thousands of dollars, then ask nothing in return.

Let's start by thanking Allen Wagner. Allen came into the office every day from the middle of March until Primary Day. He made thousands of phone calls, coordinated events, and generally did everything that was asked of him. His devotion made Dave's victory possible.

Thank you to our other faithful office volunteer, Dana Moriconi. Dana took several months off from her high-paying job to make calls, greet volunteers, and work the ground game in the Tuckahoe precinct. Dana was there every step of the way!

Ron Hedlund, owner of the AIS Liberty Dually, was a constant source of encouragement. He helped execute all the logistical items that are required to run a successful campaign but about which no one ever thinks. He drove Dave to events at a moment's notice, was a constant thorn in the side of Ray Allen, and helped keep morale up in our campaign office.

Dewey and Janet McDonnell are true patriots. They did everything from knocking on doors to organizing festivals and town halls to printing their own Dave Brat signs. Dewey and Janet are the definition of selfless.

Dewey and Janet had an excellent team in Culpeper. Chuck Duncan, Nancy Richmond, Bill Scherr, Sally Underwood, Rodney McNutt, Alexander Aitken, Eric Bierhouzen, Gene Foret, Jewell Duvall, Dale Duvall, Kurt Christensen, Stephen Cruse, Terry Osborn, Lynn and Thomas Neviaser, and William Halevy all contributed significantly to the cause in Culpeper.

Paul Shaner: You are the man. Paul knew Louisa like the back of his hand. He went door to door, worked his contacts, and did everything else in his power to ensure that Dave would win Louisa. Paul is THE reason why we won Louisa by 11 points.

Here's a huge thank-you to our Henrico County coordinators, Mark and Anita Hile. Mark and Anita worked tirelessly to recruit volunteers, knock on doors, make phone calls, and organize Election Day operations, among a million other things. Thank you!

Carolyn Worssam, our Richmond coordinator, is a pit bull. She is one of the best-educated conservatives in the state of Virginia. If a voter is persuadable, Carolyn will persuade that voter! Carolyn knocked on thousands of doors, including those of five entire precincts. And many thanks go to her faithful helper in Richmond City, Amy Hunter.

Thank you to Joe Cacciotti, Cindy Pitt Kinney, Ken Malloy, Larry Nordvig, Bill Evans, and Brian Sheldon for their hard work during the campaign.

Daryl Carr and Steve Tetrault knocked on doors six days a week from March until Primary Day. Daryl and Steve asked for nothing in return; seeing the sheer joy on their faces the night of June 10 was one awesome sight.

A huge thank-you goes to Kim Singhas, our Hanover coordinator. Kim was a part of the fight from day one, helping recruit Dave and then serving as the campaign mom. She was the 3 a.m. volunteer to whom Chris Doss refers. Kim kept the campaign on track and helped deliver a historic thumping in Hanover County. Kim is the best grassroots activist with whom we have ever worked—she will continue to be a thorn in the Establishment's side for years to come.

Dale Taylor was Kim's partner in crime. She worked countless hours behind the scenes to get Fred Gruber elected, then spent the last month of the campaign organizing volunteers to make targeted calls all over Hanover County.

The rest of our Hanover crew did absolutely outstanding work. Sally Fritzsche executed one of our key strategies. She knocked on almost every home in her neighborhood and invited neighbors to her house to meet Dave. Even those who did not attend knew the effort that Dave was making to reach out to constituents.

Herb Chittum, Larnie Allgood, Rick Ryan, Griff Durant, Beverly and Oscar Walker, Barbara Broach, Donna Bissey, Elsie Browning, John and Corrine Dixon, Mary Frances Beadles, Glenn and April Lucy, Paul Thiel, Rusty Ward, Cathy Cray, Sarah Peterson, and Janine Woods all played an integral role in delivering 63 percent of the vote in Hanover County for Dave Brat.

Major Mansfield, Bob Keeler, and Raymond Hagenbuch of the Mecahnicsville Tea Party were our sign guys. They ordered their own signs, identified excellent sign locations, installed the signs, went from door to door, and even moved their own furniture to the office.

Nancy Smith provided much-needed stability over the last month of the campaign. She came into the office almost every day and ran us through a checklist, making sure that nothing fell through the cracks. She helped edit scripts, coordinate Primary Day, and smooth things over when things got rocky.

Thank you to Susan O'Rourke in New Kent, who worked her lists and contacts to help Dave win her home precinct in commanding fashion.

Phil Rapp always did what was asked. His familiarity with our database system was a lifesaver, and his steady hand was exactly what was needed when we were about to lose our minds during the final month. Thank you, Phil.

Where would we have been in New Kent without Hannah Kraynak? Hannah made hours of phone calls every day from her home before we recruited Pete and Irene. She also went from door to door in several precincts near her home in Hanover County.

We would not have had a semblance of a campaign in Spotsylvania County had it not been for Suzanne Ircink. Suzanne spent almost every waking moment organizing Spotsylvania. Thank you to her husband, Greg Ircink, for allowing Suzanne to miss a many meal at home. God bless you Suzanne! Also, thank you to Suzanne's team in Spotsylvania: Janet and Frank Bonillo, Scott Cook, Joe Correo, Matt Rivelesse, Chris Batts, Debbie and Al Curcie, Jeanette Thomas, Charles Susler, Claude Dunn, Angelica Meecham, Michael Wood, and Kirk Twigg.

Thank you to Baird Stokes, Susan Lascolette, Margie Derrberry, and everyone else who played a role in Dave's winning Goochland County. Baird, your visits to the office were much appreciated and entertaining!

Many thanks to Dan Butler, Lisa Referson, Lynne Talley, Lisa Kyle, Rick Dodge, Dana Smith, Zach Zellner, Jean and Reed Halsted, Liz Warren, Linda Blackburn, and everyone else who did the hard work of freedom in Henrico County. It was an enormous accomplishment to win Cantor's home county.

Thank you to local radio host and longtime Cantor supporter Jim Herring for taking a stand by publicly endorsing Dave and for rounding up votes from his circle. Thank you Jim!

Our Chesterfield crew was outstanding, as evident in our convincing margin of victory in that county. Our operation was based out of Joe's Inn, led by our radio star, Ken Davis. Ken worked sixty hours a week making sure that Dave would win crucial Chesterfield. Suzanne Boukemidja was our star door knocker—she single-handedly won us hundreds of votes. Each one of the following volunteers (and we apologize to anyone we're unintentionally leaving out) played a key role in Chesterfield: Mort Coleman, Patsy Willis, Sheila and Terry Marsh, Clayton and Stephanie Gits, Jan Edens, Leanne Bowman, Lana Allen, Brian Sheldon, Frank Lehman, John Kwapijz, Jason Eggleston, Jim Robeson, Jo Billings, Beth York, Vincent Ikley, Bill Heipp, Carol Woodrum, Chris Bremer, Sue Bartlett, Tim Nester, and Dan Szabo.

Mark Ludovico is a patriot. He sits on the board of a local private school and took a stand despite the possibility of severe retribution both personally and professionally. He emailed the entire school on our behalf, as well as the members of his son's baseball league; what's more, he arranged for Dave to tour Capital One the day before the election.

Many thanks to our major donors, who took a stand against the Establishment when very few would. Don Woodsmall, Gerry Baugh, Lecia Smith, Chardon Jenks, Clayton and Stephanie Gits, Derwood Chase, Yvonne Leveque, Ron Hedlund, Russ Malone, Herb Chittum, Felix and Peggy Cross, John Gruskos, Ellen Handa,

Mr. Walter III, Cary Katz, Alfred King, Mark Mahoney, Dewey and Janet McDonnell, Sidney McVey, Gilber Meehan, Joan Peaslee, Marilyn Taylor, Kim and Gordon Singhas, Michael Vickers, George Winn, Gary Wood, and Michael Scelzi. Anyone who was willing to appear on our FEC report was a great American—and we're just sorry we don't have room to list every donor.

We are not professional writers—without Harry Stein's phenomenal editing skills, this book would not have been the polished product it now is. He spent countless hours on the project, asking for nothing in return. Harry's sense of humor is evident throughout the book. Thank you, Harry!

We are also forever indebted to Harry's wife Priscilla Turner who spent countless hours on editing and proofing the book. When there were issues with the final edit, she spent two straight days tediously fixing all the errors. Priscilla was a lifesaver.

We also want to thank the numerous people who have spent hours catching every mistake in the book: Bill and Karen Merrill, Rob Kettlewell, Theo Savory, Cary Schneider, and Grenelle Delany.

Most importantly, this victory would not have been possible without the grace of God. As Dave said on election night, the victory truly was a miracle. God blessed us with the wisdom to make the right decisions and kept us on the right course. We pray that there will be many more Dave Brat–like upsets in the coming years.

Last, we wish to thank someone who has chosen to remain anonymous lest he compromise his future effectiveness. This person's influence behind the scenes was of enormous benefit from the beginning of the campaign to its end. We will forever be grateful.

Gray

I am thankful for my parents, Peter and Grenelle Delany, for their support in the career I have chosen. They have taken a stand, risking friendships to do their part to save our country and support me. They have hosted numerous fundraisers and donated their time, money, and energy to the cause. My mom has made countless calls, worked outside polling places, and gone from door to door. She is one of the best campaigners I have ever seen, and she is extraordinarily selfless. I have been blessed!

I want to thank my sister Charlotte and my grandparents, Theo and Walt Savory, for their support and encouragement.

Chardon Jenks, a close friend, has been with me almost every step of the way in this political journey. I am grateful for her mentorship and advice. She has dedicated her life to saving the country and to preserving our freedoms. Her help during the Dave Brat campaign was invaluable.

I want to thank my former political mentor (now gone to the dark side), Dan Letovsky, for affording me the opportunity to work in politics by helping me get my first several campaign jobs. His tutelage proved invaluable. I also want to thank Dan for being exhibit A for why RINOs are despicable and need defeating.

I want to thank Mark Steyn and Peter Schweizer for their brilliant insights, which have shaped my political views. Both enlightened me to the reality of our one-party system.

Thank you to the "bench gang" in East Hampton whose lively discussions and insights have fueled my passion for politics and the conservative cause.

Thank you to my many friends who emboldened me by repeatedly saying that I am out of my mind for working on behalf of principled conservatives who are "long-shot" candidates. Because the more doubt there is, the harder I work.

A huge thank you goes out to Debbie, Billy, Emily, and Nick Agliano who welcomed me into their home, sight unseen, for the entire time that I worked on the campaign. The Aglianos became my second family. They fed me even when I came home close to midnight. Their support and generosity were much appreciated. It was a lifesaver to have a twenty minute drive to the office instead of an hour long trip from Charlottesville!

Zach

First I must thank my parents, Rick and Lori, and my little sisters Amanda and Rebecca, for always providing me a loving and supportive environment and for giving me the drive and tools I use to be successful. I also would like to thank my grandparents, Kathy, Ken, and Jeannie; my aunts and uncles, Leslie, Brad, Jen, Linda, Eric, Lisa, James, Lynn, and Donnie; and my cousins, Jeff, Eric, Sarah, Harry, Kenneth, Jack, Ava, and Ethan, for providing me with more than enough love for one person and a great foundation from which to work. I also send a special thank-you to my great grandmother, Honeybee: Thanks for giving me not just love, but insights into how the world has worked, works now, and will someday work!

Thank you to the following people from my high school years: Mr. Denny, for crystallizing my interest in leaving a mark on the world and in politics in general, and Bart Rogers and Anthony Pratley, for coaching me up in high school. Thank you also to Colin Bathory and Cory Walts in college, for instilling my grit and nearly insane focus and work ethic. Thank you to Gary Rumsey and Collins Bailey for being guides and mentors, and thank you again to Collins for letting me assist in his run for Congress against Steny Hoyer when I was only 17 years old. Thank you to Delegate Mark Berg for giving me my first political gig, thank you to Christopher Doss for taking me under his wing, and thank you to Morton Blackwell for the Leadership Institute, without which none of this could have been possible.

Finally, thank you to my best friend, Scott Chanelli, who, after my desperate pleas with just ten days left in the campaign, drove up from North Carolina to help Gray and me deal with the sheer chaos in our campaign office. Scott, you risked a new job to help me in my hour of need and were unafraid to stand in front of the locomotive with me. Such behavior cannot go without the heartiest of thanks.

Made in the USA
San Bernardino, CA
07 January 2016